Reading and Responding to Poetry

Reading and Responding to Poetry
Patterns in the Process

Patrick X. Dias

Boynton/Cook Publishers
HEINEMANN
Portsmouth, NH

Boynton/Cook Publishers
A subsidiary of Reed Elsevier Inc.
361 Hanover Street
Portsmouth, NH 03801-3912

Offices and agents throughout the world

Earlier edition published in 1987 by the Canadian Council of Teachers of English

"Blackberry-Picking" by Seamus Heaney, copyright © 1966, 1969, 1972, 1975, 1980 by Seamus Heaney, reprinted by permission of Faber and Faber Limited from *Death of a Naturalist* by Seamus Heaney and by permission of Farrar, Straus and Giroux, Inc., from *Poems 1965–1975* by Seamus Heaney.

"Cyclops" by Margaret Atwood, copyright © 1970 by Margaret Atwood and reprinted by permission of Oxford University Press Canada and Margaret Atwood from *Procedures for Underground.*

Library of Congress Cataloging-in-Publication Data
CIP is on file with the Library of Congress.
0-86709-372-2

Editor: Peter Stillman
Production: Renée Le Verrier, Melissa L. Inglis
Cover design: Darci Mehall

Printed in the United States of America on acid-free paper.
98 97 96 95   DA   1 2 3 4 5 6

Contents

Preface

The present edition of *Reading and Responding to Poetry* is revised from an earlier one only to the extent that I have, in some places, qualified or elaborated on earlier comments, provided supplementary information, and updated some references. In Chapter Five, which is concerned with the classroom implications of this study, I have added several paragraphs to expand on those implications. As I have continued to work in the area of response to literature and discussed my work with teachers K–12 and beyond, I have benefited from considerable feedback, which will be apparent in my reflections in that closing chapter.

It also became apparent to me that the *Making Sense* in the original title, *Making Sense of Poetry*, had registered with some readers as emphasizing comprehension of the literal meaning of poems at the expense of their affective-aesthetic aspects. In changing the title of the book to *Reading and Responding to Poetry*, I intend to correct such a misapprehension, hoping at the same time that *Reading and Responding* will still convey the idea that readers are involved in an "effort after meaning" (I borrow the phrase from F. C. Bartlett's pioneering study, *Remembering*, 1932). For reading and responding to poetry in schools, it turns out, is hardly effortless, and often without pleasure, which has much to do with how certain classroom practices have defined poetry and poetry reading. I hope the reissue of this work contributes in some way toward the redefinition of our goals and practices in teaching a genre that ought to form an essential core of any curriculum in literature.

Acknowledgments

The present edition provides an opportunity to reiterate several thank yous. I remain grateful to all the people mentioned in the earlier edition's Acknowledgments section, which is reprinted below, and would like to add here my gratitude to Bob Boynton and Peter Stillman, who believed this book merited a wider readership and supported its new publication.

I gratefully acknowledge as well the support of my students, my colleagues, and the hundreds of teachers with whom I have shared this work, especially those in Manitoba, New Brunswick, Newfoundland, Nova Scotia, Ontario and Quebec (my home province), and in the United States, in Alaska, California, and Ohio.

Above all, my wife, Patricia, and my children, Catherine, John, George, and Andrew, have been patient listeners and survivors.

I dedicated the earlier edition of this book to my brother George in Pakistan. He was delighted by this gesture. Just over a year after its publication, he died tragically in the country where he had served the poor and sick with dedication for twenty-six years. George, this again is for you.

November 1994

Several people have contributed in various ways to the completion of this study. The prime contributors are of course the pupils of Laval Catholic High School, Laval, Quebec, who were such wonderful collaborators and who taught me a great deal about the real abilities of pupils as readers. I do not believe I would have pursued this study with such enthusiasm if I had not been urged on by their teacher, Alan Patenaude, who saw the worth of the study and eased my way through the administrative and organizational groundwork. For always extending such an easy entry to their school and for taking the time to schedule pupils and rooms, I am indebted to Principal Bernard Lemieux and to Mr. Armand Laderoute, Director of Studies.

Throughout this study, I have spoken as though I were the sole investigator, without reference to the efforts of Anthony Paré and Carolyn Pittenger, who assisted me in carrying out the study, analyzing the protocols, and preparing the final report. They helped me considerably in identifying the four patterns of reading that this study describes. Most readers will recognize my debt to Louise Rosenblatt, whose work has inspired the spirit and direction of my inquiry. I am grateful as well to Martin O'Hara, former departmental chairman, continuing friend and mentor, who encouraged me by example and instances; to Anthony Adams of the University of Cambridge, for his enthusiastic response when he first observed the small-group work at Laval Catholic High School in 1979; to Ian Pringle, who encouraged me to develop my study for publication; to colleagues Frank Greene and Mary Maguire, who provided useful feedback; to Patti de Verteuil, who did the painstaking work of transcribing the individual and small-group protocols; to the several readers who helped confirm my readings of the protocols: Sharon Asher, Juliet Dunphy, Patricia Gordon, Eva Hadjis, Beryl Parker, and Penny Ross. I am grateful as well to the teachers and my students who have heard my accounts of the patterns, encouraged me by their confirmatory reactions, and sharpened my account by their questions and observations.

This study was supported by a grant from the Social Sciences and Humanities Research Council of Canada. Supplementary funding was provided by McGill University's Social Sciences Research Grants Committee. Parts of Chapters One and Two have appeared in the *English Quarterly*; the feedback provided by the editors and several anonymous readers has been most useful in preparing this manuscript.

I promised my brother George in Pakistan, who has always kept me in his prayers, that I would dedicate my first book to him. This is it, Father George.

March, 1987

Reading and Responding to Poetry

Introduction

This study seeks to answer the question, What happens in the transaction between adolescent readers and poems? I use the term *transaction* in Louise Rosenblatt's sense of the term, as "an active process lived through during the relationship between a reader and a text" (1978, 20–21). The question is important. As teachers, we too often proceed as though our students approach and read poetry with the same set of expectations, and are involved in the same kinds of processes, as we are when we read poetry. The gap we see between their readings and ours we tend to attribute to inexperience and not to differences in approach and process. Our teaching needs to be informed by knowledge of the processes by which our adolescent readers make sense of poetry (and other literary genres, for that matter) so that we are less often working at cross-purposes.

How *do* adolescent readers make sense of poetry? That was not exactly how I framed my question when I first began inquiring about adolescent response to poetry almost twenty years ago. At that time, I had been concerned about the growing antipathy to poetry among secondary school students, an antipathy often acquiesced to in the decreasing amount of poetry included in secondary school programs and an increasing reluctance on the part of many teachers to teach poetry. I became aware of this growing reluctance primarily during my supervision of practice teaching. More and more of the student teachers I supervised in secondary schools were being asked by the veteran teachers if they would be willing to teach the poetry portion of the literature program.

I hypothesized at that time that students' antipathy to poetry arose essentially from their belief that they could not make sense of and appreciate a poem unless a teacher mediated that process. I believed that teachers had in effect taken responsibility for making sense of poetry away from the students.

Teachers would find it quite reasonable to expect students to read and make sense of a short story or a novel on their own; however, rarely, if ever, were students assigned responsibility for reading, and still less for understanding, poems on their own. Reading poetry was, in fact, primarily and essentially a teacher-directed classroom activity. It seemed to me at the time that the cause of poetry in the secondary school curriculum would be aided considerably if teachers and their students could come to believe that students had within themselves the capabilities for making sense of poetry on their own, but that these capabilities would emerge only if they were properly and frequently exercised. I had, however, to find some evidence for such an argument.

I did so by involving a class of sixteen-year-olds in undirected small-group discussion of poetry over a period of two weeks and monitoring their performance by several means. That study (Dias 1979) provided convincing evidence that high school students could be relied on to realize a poem for themselves and that undirected small-group discussion is a powerful procedure for helping students to become independent readers of poetry. Moreover, there was good reason to believe that students could without undue difficulty overcome their antipathy to poetry. I describe the procedure I devised for that study later in this book. That procedure is a key feature in the design of this study.

I believe I had demonstrated that adolescents were far more capable as readers of poetry than was acknowledged by some of the teacher-dominated approaches in many English classrooms; however, that study had thrown up many questions whose answers I could only guess at. Transcripts of the small-group discussions that I had recorded gave some hints as to the processes by which readers can collaboratively create meaning; but the process appeared to be largely one of chance intuitions and fortuitous turns of thought. Some readers in the group appeared to be more successful than others in making the kinds of observations that keep discussion going and allow for new realizations; other seemingly unsuccessful readers made key contributions. By what processes had these readers arrived at the meanings they offered to the group? If that question were even partially answered, classroom practices might work in consonance with those processes rather than be indifferent to them or even, at worst, oppose them.

Not enough is known about the processes by which readers make sense of poetry for there to be any clear consensus as to which teaching practices assist or inhibit the process of reading a poem. While the close-reading emphasis of New Criticism is no longer influential in critical theory and practice, teaching practice still appears to be dominated by approaches that focus primarily on textual meaning and close reading: a poem is an object to be analyzed, an object that will reveal its full meaning only when its complex inner workings are explained. The question for most teachers is still, to borrow the title of the poet John Ciardi's monograph (1959), How does a poem mean? rather than How do readers mean? While the former question remains important and has enjoyed considerable play, the latter, with a few exceptions, has hardly been asked, especially with regard to poetry. Thus I framed the questions that directed this study:

- What occurs in the transaction between adolescent readers and a poem?
- How do these individuals differ in the ways they go about making sense of poetry? Can there be discerned in their transactions with a poem clearly identifiable individual patterns of reading?

In the following pages I report on the inquiry I undertook. I discuss briefly in Chapter One the status of what is currently argued in theory and research on response to literature and then go on in Chapter Two to describe the methodology I devised for this study. Chapter Three presents some of the data arising from the procedures used in this study. Of special interest are the texts of four readers' responses to Seamus Heaney's "Blackberry-Picking." In Chapter Four, I propose a list of elements involved in making sense of a poem. Perhaps the most interesting section of the chapter describes the kinds of readers of poetry I have discerned in the readers' protocols and considers how the elements help distinguish patterns of reading. Chapter Five explains the implications of the findings for classroom practices, provides examples of the kind of teaching strategies that are consistent with the findings of this study, and goes on to suggest the directions in which further research on response to literature might proceed.

This study addresses two related, though at times divergent, concerns. The first is, To what extent do current research methodologies on response to literature really penetrate to the process involved in the transaction between adolescent reader and literary text? A second and major concern is to share with teachers and researchers the accounts of reading patterns deriving from this study and to offer for classroom practice suggestions that take account of these patterns and their differences. Readers who are most interested in methodology and teaching implications may want to begin with Chapter Three and continue from there, returning to the earlier chapters when they have found sufficient justification for reading them.

Readers should also know that this study reports primarily on one aspect of the process of responding to poetry: the process by which readers make sense of literary text. Instructions given to the students in the study focused on "making sense" or "reporting on your understanding." From my earlier work, it was clear to me that "making sense" and "understanding poetry" are the goals that adolescent readers set themselves when asked to read a poem and report on their response. In contrast, an instruction to "report on your response or your experience of the poem" would suggest a passivity that is not in keeping with the active role readers assume before literary text. Thus, while the procedures described in this study do not rule out readers' reporting on their evocation of the poem, on the "lived-through experience of the work" (Rosenblatt 1978), I feel this study emphasizes the processes involved in *reading* poetry rather than in responding to it. I do not see this as a constraining of the study's goals; rather, the study provides a window on those initial encounters with poetic text that account to a considerable extent for what is evoked and what is lived through.

The British literary critic F. R. Leavis often said that he offered his critical views with the implied question, This is so, isn't it? and always understood that his readers (and students) could respond, Yes, but . . . . In my presentations of the results of this research at several meetings of English teachers, I had the encouragement of many corroborating nods; I hope this much fuller account will also occasion the "Yes, buts . . ." that will help clarify and define what are but tentative positions in a rather crucial area.

1

Studies of Response to Literature

Discussions of response to literature compose a substantial academic enterprise. It is a field that has the attention of literary theorists and critics, of researchers in reading and discourse analysts, and of researchers in the teaching of English. In this brief survey of such work I shall discuss only those issues that pertain directly to the questions set for this study.

Response and Literary Criticism

When we examine literary critical writing that bears directly on response to literature, we find, over the last two decades especially, a shift from a close study of literary text toward an increasing emphasis on the role of the reader in making sense of literature. Concomitant with the attention to readers is a growing interest in the contexts from which a literary work derives and the contexts within which it is read: hence the importation into the study of literature of, for instance, speech-act theory, semiotics, pragmatics, phenomenology, psychology, feminist theory, and discourse theory. Suleiman and Crossman's collection of articles on the role of the reader (1980) and Tompkins' *Reader-response Criticism: From Formalism to Post-structuralism* (1980) give a fair picture of the widening scope of such studies, and William Slatoff's clever title *With Respect to Readers: Dimensions of Literary Response* (1970) plainly (and early) announces the new emphasis.[1] Of course, interest in the role of readers is not entirely new, as I. A. Richards' pioneering work in describing sources of difficulty in the reading of poetry (1929) demonstrates. At the heart of such shifts is the understanding, as Leavis puts

1. Griffith's *Literary Theory and English Teaching* (1987), and Richard Beach's *A Teacher's Introduction to Reader-Response Theories* (1993) provide more recent accounts of developments in reader-response theory.

5

it, that one "cannot point to the poem, it is 'there' only in the recreative response of the individual to the black marks on the page" (1962, 28).

And yet, although such work has moved our understanding of response to literature considerably forward (and because it has done so), one is aware of some limitations that justify inquiry of the kind undertaken in this study.

In the first place, literary critical inquiry has worked essentially from the responses of educated and informed adults, and with the needs of an informed readership in mind. Such readings have an aura of the ideal about them; yet in much pedagogical practice they have represented models for imitation by less informed and adolescent readers. Even where such inquiry has dwelled specifically on reader response, the responses examined are those of quite articulate and critically aware students of literature: Kintgen (1983), for instance. Phenomenological criticism (Iser 1978), psychoanalytic and subjective criticism (Holland 1973; 1975; Bleich 1975; 1978), structuralist and post-structuralist criticism (Culler 1975; 1981)[2] develop their arguments mainly on the basis of the critics' introspective accounts of their own quite attentive readings or of the readings of graduate students of literature who appear to be well-motivated and alert. If such work has any bearing on the reading processes of younger, inexperienced readers of literature, it does so only to the extent that the work of expert readers may be said to illuminate the efforts of novice readers.

In the second place, because these accounts are essentially introspective, I must question the extent to which they reflect the processes of responding to literature. I recognize that important information about the responding process can be inferred from such written products. However, in that these responses are in writing, they represent more the end product of the responding process than they do the process itself. As written products, they must to some extent both be directed by whatever demands are imposed by the writing context and at the same time be faithful to the response as it registers. I shall return to this point when I discuss the design of my study and explain why I sought oral rather than written responses to poetry.

Response and Research in Reading and Discourse Analysis

Research in the fields of reading and discourse analysis displays similarly a shift from the study of reading with the text viewed as a stable entity to the study of reading "as a language process involving flexible interactions among the reader, the text, and the context in which the meaning is derived" (Langer and Smith-Burke 1982, vii). The notion that meaning does not reside entirely in the text, that the reader also brings meaning to the text, has led to signifi-

2. See also Belsey (1980); Eagleton (1983); Mailloux (1982).

cant developments in reading research and discourse analysis (paralleling similar developments in literary critical thinking). This recognition of the transactional nature of the act of reading is clearly apparent in the emergence of some key concepts that have been used to explain how readers process text: schemata and macrostructures (Anderson 1977; van Dijk 1980), frames (Minsky 1975), scripts (Schank and Abelson 1977), and scenarios (Sanford and Garrod 1981). Generally they refer to ways of representing background knowledge, "conceptual configurations" (Dillon 1980, 164) used by the reader to meaningfully organize material in a text.

Much of such research, however, continues to focus on discursive prose. Where reading research has been concerned with literary texts, it has dealt with specific issues such as the processing of metaphorical language or the effects of specific interventions on comprehension, or with the effects of teaching particular literary devices on the appreciation of literature. I cite such examples not to dismiss their usefulness, but merely to point out that such research does not really address the question of what happens during the act of reading a literary work. Where reading research has attended to the process of reading a literary text, it has done so, as in the research of Olshavsky (1976/77), by asking readers to stop and report on their responses at pre-set pauses in the story (in this case, after each independent clause), a procedure that is likely to seriously distort the process of reading a story. Again, such research has stayed clear of dealing with the processing of poetry. Even where narrative prose is involved, the passages are usually short, especially written to meet experimental demands, and of little or no literary value.[3] Thus, for instance, those who study story understanding experimentally have tended to emphasize "the mechanically analytic" and to ignore the "experiential aspects of text comprehension" (Spiro 1982, 78). Again, as Dillon puts it, "the conventions governing laboratory experiments in memory and summary are rather unlike those governing many situations in which literature is read" (1980, 164). Dillon has in mind the "story recall" tasks that are the staple of many discourse-processing studies. He goes on to say,

> A commonly expressed twentieth-century view of literature is that it involves the deautomization of experience, and it is just this aspect of the reading of literary narrative that is most obscured by the laboratory model of "normal" narrative processing. (1980, 178)

It seems that any research that hopes to deal realistically with the processing of literary text must first ensure that readers are in a position to access the strategies and skills they would call on in the normal process of reading a story or a poem. In designing this study, I gave prime consideration to ensuring a setting that assists rather than inhibits the reading of a poem and the

---

3. Russel Hunt (1993) aptly refers to such texts as "textoids."

articulation of a response. Moreover, despite the reservations I have about such research, I took advantage of several insights from reading research and discourse-processing theory. This is particularly apparent in my discussion of the elements that helped me chart the patterns of response I put forward in Chapter Four.

Response and Research in the Teaching of English

Surveys of educational research in the area of response to literature record a wide variety of work, particularly over the last two decades (Cooper, ed. 1985; Klemenz-Belgardt 1981; Applebee 1977; D'Arcy 1973; Purves and Beach 1972; Cooper 1971).[4] Such work has focused variously on the process of responding itself, on identifying elements of readers' responses to literature, on the factors involved in understanding literature and the difficulties readers encounter, on the factors influencing readers' judgments of literature, on the effects of a variety of instructional strategies on student response, on the development of response over time, and on the relationships of a variety of factors such as age, gender, attitude, the nature of the literary work itself, and the contexts in which the work is read. Such studies have largely used school-age and college-level students and because of their pedagogical concerns pertain directly to the concerns of this study.

As with much of the work in literary criticism, discourse analysis, and reading, there are as well here, in most of these studies, serious grounds for questioning whether the data-collecting methods really penetrate to the complex process of responding to literature. Many of these data are in the form of written accounts of individuals' responses to literary works, these responses having been obtained by inviting subjects to write freely about a particular work, to keep logs of their responses as they read, or to write in response to specific questions. Such accounts cannot be said to represent, immediately and directly, the process by which a reader makes sense of a literary work. For most school- and college-age writers, I would argue, the medium of writing is itself an interposition between their immediate and developing response and their expression of it, despite whatever else may be said for the claims of writing as a process that enables one to record, develop, and clarify one's response. For instance, Travers, examining the response of one fourteen-year-old pupil who was asked to think aloud as he wrote about a poem for thirty minutes, is struck by his inability "to convey anything of his fluent and perceptive response in writing" (1982, 64).

Again, such responses are largely retrospective accounts of the process the reader has just gone through. They represent more likely the end results of a process than the process itself. It is Applebee's view, for instance, that most

4. Recent developments are recorded by Beach and Hynds (1990), who list over two hundred such studies published in English since 1970; more than 35 percent of these studies have been published since 1985. See also Beach and Hynds (1991) and Beach (1993).

such studies "have treated 'response' as something static, occurring in a fixed and measurable form after exposure to a literary work . . . an oversimplification of the complex and little-understood process which produces this final response" (1977, 261). Yet I must admit that some researchers have sought to obtain written responses by designing questions that respect or at least do not constrain the process of responding (for example, LATE 1968), and that despite these limitations, studies based on written responses have produced useful insights into the process (Cooper, ed. 1985; Rosenblatt 1978; Purves with Rippere 1968; Richards 1929).

Oral responses to literature, freed as they are from the constraints of writing, are certainly more immediate and direct than written responses. Applebee (1978), for instance, found that the oral responses of nine-year-olds were longer than their written responses and involved more retelling and less summarization. Squire, in an attempt "to record the thought processes of readers during the complete act of responding to a story," interviewed his subjects (nondirectively) at several pre-set breaks in their reading of a short story (1964, 16). Holland (1975), who uses a psychoanalytic approach to the study of response, had his subjects read a story and reflect on their reading prior to their being interviewed. Holland sees the reader as all important and the text "as a relatively neutral phenomenon," as Purves (1979), puts it; in addition, he appears to be interested in the end product of reading, in his readers' retellings, rather than in whether they recall their experiences of the text accurately. Free, unstructured response, though highly desirable, is at the same time not easily amenable to analysis, especially where large samples are involved. Thus one part of the National Assessment of Educational Progress study of response to literature (1973), which involved over fourteen thousand samples of response, depended on "channelling questions" to elicit oral responses. These questions made it possible to assign answers to one of the four major categories in the list of Purves' elements of response (Purves with Rippere 1968).

It is the need to produce findings that can be generalized that has made response to literature such a problematic area of research. Many researchers believe that responding situations involve too many variables that cannot be held constant. Attempts to reduce such variables and find objective measures of the responding process end up reporting not so much on the responding process itself as on the outcomes of that process, e.g., the judgments readers make about a literary work and the criteria they bring to these judgments (Britton 1954; Harpin 1966; Harding 1968). By far the most ambitious study, *Literature Education in Ten Countries*, sponsored by the International Association for the Evaluation of Educational Achievement (Purves et al. 1973), examines the response patterns of students in ten different countries. Of particular interest is its attempt to establish a reliable instrument "to identify and measure important dimensions of aesthetic response" (p. 9). In its attempt to be objective, however, the instrument limits the range of responses to those covered by the test items, inviting readers to identify their preferred responses by choosing from among these items. John Mellon (1975, 85) sums up the concerns I have expressed so far:

> Foremost of these is the fact that the primary data of response remain unconscious in the mind of the reader. What is accessible to introspection is a confused jumble, only fragments of which can ever be externalized verbally. And even if introspective data or "inner speech" could be gotten out and recorded, they would constitute but the tip of an iceberg with respect to the unconscious conceptual and judgmental processing performed by the mind whenever any verbal discourse is received, whether or not it is literary in form. Other practical research problems also appear. Multiple-choice questions force the reader to select the best of another's responses to the work in question rather than one's own. Open-ended essay questions allow full freedom for the expression of response, but impose the additional burden that the persons answering must compose their responses in some organized fashion. Broadly speaking, they must in effect produce one literary work in response to another literary work, and in so doing must strike off from the original work in any one of an indefinite number of possible directions, more or less ignoring all the others.

If reader-response research is to be more truly reflective of the processes it studies, it must avoid several of the foregoing constraints and at the same time ensure that the effort to remove such constraints does not itself distort the actual process of responding or transform it in any way. Such research, therefore, must depend largely on oral response for its immediacy and fluency. Oral reporting is not as free from constraints as one would hope. While it is certainly more immediate, the interview situation itself might inhibit or overly direct response. Furthermore, such responses must be freed from the demands of teacher expectations, implicit or otherwise. Above all, researchers should be at considerable effort to tap such responses as they occur rather than depend on retrospective accounts for their data. In Chapter Two I describe procedures for a study that attempts to take account of such constraints.

2

Tapping Response to Poetry

In surveying the wide variety of work on response to literature, I was concerned primarily to discover those procedures that might provide access to the responding processes of adolescent readers. In most of the research I examined, the data collection procedures focused on retrospective accounts, end products of the act of responding rather than the process as it occurs. In such cases, as Stanley Fish puts it (1980, 375), what we get is a response to a response rather than the actual response itself. I also argued that even in those studies that were concerned to obtain response as it occurs, the research procedures may have constrained the reading process to the extent that the data obtained might not represent what actually occurs in encounters between readers and literary texts. Of course, any such research procedures import some artificiality into the reading situation; and it should be a concern in such studies to minimize such effects. Thus I was concerned to design a study that would

- Tap response as it occurs
- Reduce the constraints that might inhibit readers' responses and their articulation of those responses
- Recognize that the readers involved are inexperienced adolescent readers of poetry, most likely inhibited about responding to poetry and ruled by school-conditioned expectations about what one says and does not say when asked to respond to a poem
- Furnish supplementary data in order to provide a more comprehensive base for the analysis that must follow.

The method described here is particular to the reading of poetry; with some modifications, I believe the procedure can be applied to drawing out responses to short fiction as well.

The method is predicated on a number of assumptions concerning the validity of verbal responses as data, and the potential of undirected small-group discussion for developing confident readers of literature and also for providing a record of the dynamic process of responding to literature.

The Act of Reading and Responding to Poetry

A basic assumption of this method is that the act of reading a literary work is one of actively construing meaning from the text. "Words in poetry invite us, not to 'think about' and judge but to 'feel into' or 'become'—to realize a complex experience given in the words" (Leavis 1963, 212–213). As L. C. Knights puts it (1964, 77), the poet in a variety of ways enlists "the active collaboration of the reader" in realizing the experience given in the words:

> In varied ways the mind's energies are evoked and directed in a single "realizing intuition." In the larger works, of course, the scope is wider and the perceptions are likely to be related in more complex ways . . . . Routine notions and attitudes are broken down, and a new direction of consciousness emerges from the interplay of meanings: not meanings, so to speak, "out there," as though we were trying to understand a legal document, but meanings, in which the reader or spectator is involved as a person, simply because movements of sympathy or antipathy, of assent or dissent—in short, of judgement from a personal centre—are a necessary part of them.

The reader's involvement as a person implies that a response will reflect the reader's cognitive style and his or her cultural and social norms, attitudes, and expectations. All the more reason then that attempts to make sense of pupils' responses to poetry must take account of data other than just the verbal records of those responses.

A second assumption, and a source of major difficulty in charting response to poetry, is that the apprehension of a poem involves a complex organic process that cannot be reduced to a set of subskills. Neither is it a linear process proceeding from simple to complex or from wholes to elements. Richard Young speaks of the literary work as

> a complex system functioning within the mind of the reader . . . . Understanding the theme, and in some sense the meaning of the work as a whole, requires the apprehension of a semantic field that relates the parts to each other and to the world beyond the work. . . . It [the theme] is not a part of the work or all the parts taken together; it is a relational principle that emerges out of the reader's active involvement with the text. (1986, 315)

D. W. Harding sees the reading of a poem as a highly complex task. It includes construing the bare sense of the poem; perceiving relations among its various features; inferring attitudes implied by the author; relating all that the poet conveys to the reader's own structure of values; observing the effectiveness with which language is used (1968, 3–4).

Any method designed to elicit response to poetry can only *begin* to take account of the complex demands made on the reader.

Verbal Reports as Data

Because I was concerned to record response to poetry while that response occurred and registered, and because I believe that seeking a written response to a poem might constrain the reporting on that process, this study draws on oral response for its data. Ericsson and Simon (1980; 1984) make a convincing case for the validity of verbal reports as data—not verbal reports that call for retrospective information leading to subjects' inferring their mental processes, but verbal reports obtained by asking subjects to say what they are thinking while engaged in the activity under examination.[1] Linda Flower and John Hayes (Flower and Hayes 1985; Hayes and Flower 1980; 1983) in developing their "thinking aloud" approach to gathering data on the writing process, have demonstrated that such an approach provides rich information on the cognitive processes involved in writing. While such a claim has been disputed by some who doubt the ecological validity of the approach (e.g., Cooper and Holzman 1983), I am inclined to believe that Flower and Hayes are not blind to the limitations of their approach: they suggest that think-aloud protocols provide an incomplete record but at the same time a useful window on the writing process.

Y. Waern (1979), of the University of Stockholm, has developed a similar approach to investigating the reading processes of subjects reading a short piece of expository prose. John Hayes and his colleagues at Carnegie Mellon University have also used readers' think-aloud protocols to discover what portions of a text might present difficulties to readers.

The extension of such an approach to readers' reporting on their processing of a poem is logical and promising. Readers are invited by the interviewer simply to think aloud as they work their way through a poem in as many readings as they feel are necessary to make sense of the poem. The process is tape-recorded for later transcription and analysis. I do not wish to argue that these responding-aloud protocols report accurately and fully on the process that is being verbalized. Admittedly, there is much that is likely to remain tacit and unarticulated. I am convinced, however, for the following reasons, that think-aloud methodology can provide substantial data on the process of responding to a poem. First, the verbalization is close to being concurrent with the responding, though not necessarily identical with it. Second, "making sense of a poem" and verbalizing that process are interdependent activities: the verbalization that occurs is not apart from the process of making sense and most likely facilitates the "effort after meaning," to use F. C. Bartlett's phrase (1932). Third, critics of think-aloud protocols argue that one cannot report

1. See also Afflerbach and Johnston (1984); Smagorinsky (1989).

faithfully on the process one is involved in without in some way altering that process. Does verbalizing one's thinking interfere with the way one normally works at making sense of poetry? I would argue that particularly with poetry, thinking aloud in the process of making sense of the text is not necessarily inconsistent with the process of responding to a poem. If anything, it assists rather than inhibits the process of responding. Also, students normally expect to reflect aloud and verbalize their understanding of a poem (even if it is only in response to the usual classroom questions, like Now, what do you think? and Does anyone have any thoughts about this poem?); so it is not unusual to ask pupils to verbalize their working toward that understanding. And certainly, compared to other methods used to obtain responses to poetry (writing retrospectively and introspectively, interviews, free writing, for instance), think-aloud protocols are less of an interference. In regard to the use of think-aloud protocols for writing and problem-solving research, it seems to me that it is less difficult to read and think aloud than it is to write or play chess (as in some problem-solving research) and think aloud. Nor do responding-aloud protocols require recoding information from one medium to another, for instance, contemplating a particular move in chess, then verbalizing about it.

It is probable that the responding-aloud procedure would not be as successful (paradoxically) with expert readers of poetry. We may be unable to derive information on some basic and intermediate stages in the process of making sense of poetry simply because, for these readers, these stages may have become automatic and thus unnoticed. This is unlikely to have occurred with our readers. (Fish's method for slowing down "the reading experience so that 'events' one does not notice in normal time, but which do occur, are brought before our analytical attentions" [1980, 28] may have some merit here if we are considering exploring the processes of expert readers.)

The responding-aloud protocols I obtained confirm that the invitation to think aloud while reading is easily taken up; words flow, and there is little uncertainty among these readers as to what they are expected to do. Much of this facility derives, I am convinced, from the activities that preceded the protocol collection sessions, and that is the point of the following assumption.

The Potential of Undirected Small-Group Discussion of Poetry

Small-group discussions are a means of developing confident readers of poetry. As I argued in the Introduction, for most adolescents the reading of poetry, unlike the reading of fiction, is seen as a school activity. These students have grown up with the expectation that poetry will make sense only with the intervention of the teacher, who either asks the right questions or provides timely directives and explanations. The expectation that most adolescent readers can read and make sense of fiction on their own is well founded—most adult readers are hard put to explain where and how they learned to read fiction. There is no question, however, that most of them will recall repeated attempts to learn how to read poetry and remember these essentially as classroom, teacher-directed activities. They will also most likely confess that they are as yet unable to make sense of poetry on their own.

Several factors explain why students do not function as independent readers as far as poetry is concerned. Such readers are unlikely to reveal the processes by which they make sense of poetry primarily because they do not expect to make sense of poetry on their own. A solution is suggested by a study reporting on the effectiveness of undirected small-group discussion as a means of developing independent readers of poetry (Dias 1979). The study, involving small groups in generally undirected discussion of poetry over ten sessions, realized significant gains in the ability of the group members (mostly sixteen-year-olds) to read and apprehend poetry independently. Transcripts of the discussions reveal improved attention to the text and a desire to arrive at meaning through a process largely tentative, exploratory, and essentially collaborative. The results of this study have been borne out by a replication (Bryant 1984).[2]

The students' active involvement in the text, their facility in articulating response, their concerted effort after meaning, and the conviction that meaning will be arrived at, all make undirected small-group discussion a promising means of developing autonomous readers of poetry who can speak with some confidence in their ability to make sense of poetry when asked to think aloud during the responding-aloud sessions. What is most important for this study is that the students who were involved in such small-group discussions appeared gradually to take responsibility for making sense of the poem and were therefore less likely to be directed by school-derived expectations of how they must talk about a poem. The small-group discussion transcripts from my own earlier preparatory studies show a gradual development of autonomous behavior among the students involved: a confidence in their own responses, the emergence of individual strategies, tolerance of ambiguity, a tentativeness about meaning, and a willingness to change their minds. The reading-aloud protocols, following on the group discussions, were expected to elicit patterns of response that may not have been available in the teacher-dominated approach to literature used in many classrooms.

Small-group discussions are also a source of data.

The undirected small-group discussion procedure described here allowed students over a ten-session period to develop a high degree of confidence in their ability to read and apprehend poetry. While this report deals primarily with the individual responding-aloud protocols and what they reveal about

2. I have presented the approach in several workshops yearly and have received several confirming reports that bear out its effectiveness with students of varying ability from grade two to university and in adult education classes. For published reports see Engbrecht (1986); Straw (1989); and most recently, Krogness (1994).

patterns of response to poetry, the discussion that follows is intended to point out the potential of small-group discussion transcripts as a source of additional and corroborative data on the processes involved in making sense of literature. The discussion is included here because data from the small-group discussions have proved useful in confirming the patterns revealed in the individual protocols.

The potential of undirected small-group discussion as a record of the dynamic process of responding has yet to be exploited in any concerted way. Part of Beach's (1972) study of the responses of college students to poetry does consider patterns of response during small-group discussion of three poems, but in a limited way. The small-group discussion was used primarily to register the effects of written or taped free-association responses to the poem rather than merely the effects of reading the poem. In England there have been several classroom experiments with undirected small-group discussion of literature (Barnes, Churley, and Thompson 1971; Stratta, Dixon, and Wilkinson 1973; Dixon 1974; Mills 1974; Torbe 1974; Grugeon and Walden 1978) intended mainly to demonstrate the pedagogical effectiveness of this approach, to provide instances of "learning through talk."[3] From the samples of the discussions reproduced in such work, it becomes clear that undirected small-group discussion might provide useful data on the responding process. It is also apparent from these accounts that undirected small-group discussion represents a pedagogical approach more fully consistent with current literary critical notions of the process of reading and responding to a literary work than are most teacher-directed approaches (e.g., Culler 1981; Suleiman and Crossman 1980; Rosenblatt 1978).

M. J. L. Abercrombie's study of the process by which small groups in free discussion (medical students, in this case) arrive at judgment provides further support for the procedures advocated by this study:

> It may legitimately be stressed that in free group discussion techniques there lies a promising tool for investigating those hidden processes of our own and other people's thinking which so powerfully govern our behaviour, and about which we know so little. (1969, 98)

Richards (1929) and Squire (1964) have clearly established that there are several difficulties that tend to obtrude on an individual's reading of a poem. It remains to be seen to what extent group discussion procedures reduce the effects of these difficulties (for instance, "critical predispositions" and reliance on stock responses), but some gains will certainly emerge. The group discussion procedure (if past experience is sufficient guide) should establish a

---

3. In the years since this study was published, there have appeared several studies on the value of group work in the study of literature, including poetry. Especially worth attention are Barnes and Barnes (1990); Benton et al. (1988); Eeds and Wells (1989); Langer (1992); and Willinsky (1990). Brubacher, Payne, and Rickett (1990) provide a particularly well-balanced perspective on cooperative and collaborative learning.

process of attending to the text itself rather than being directed by preconceptions about the text. It should allow individuals to work through and beyond personal associations to become tolerant of ambiguity, and to pay more attention to the contributions of other members of the group. It confirms to the students that the process of collaborative discussion can be fruitfully engaged in and that the search for meaning is only as productive as it is collaborative.

The Design of the Study

Population

The study involved two groups of approximately twenty-five students each at the grade 9 and grade 10 levels, corresponding to age levels 15 to 15,11 and 16 to 16,11, in a large semiurban comprehensive school. Socioeconomically, the students were mainly from middle-income working-class families. At least two thirds of the students were children of first-generation non-English-speaking immigrants. Because the study sought to find out how adolescents read poems, I thought it best to work with pupils of average ability so that findings would have wider applicability than if they had been confined to low or high ability groups. In both classes the pupils had read very little poetry in class or outside, and were, according to their teachers, generally antipathetic or, at best, indifferent to poetry. The two classes represented the middle third of approximately 275 students at each of their grade levels and were identified with their teachers' assistance on the basis of overall achievement in their previous grade level, and on achievement in tests involving comprehension of a short story and a poem. On the same basis, a middle group of six students was identified from among them as the target group in each class. The target groups were made up equally of boys and girls and were fairly representative of the larger school population.

The twelve students in the target groups were the main subjects of this study. They provided the protocols from which my accounts of their reading processes derive.

Materials

For the small-group sessions I used several unfamiliar modern poems, appropriate to the grade level, not necessarily all linked thematically, and of a length appropriate for a one-session discussion.

Four unfamiliar poems of appropriate length and difficulty were used in the responding-aloud sessions. These poems were sufficiently different to allow them to be considered independently, with only a slight chance that associations and meaning would carry over from one poem to another.

The selections, equally divided among poems by contemporary British and Canadian poets, were from several anthologies designed for use in secondary schools. Their appropriateness for use in this study was confirmed by several high school teachers of English whom I consulted. I was assured that the students were unlikely to have read these poems before. There were also no indications during the study that the pupils had seen any of the poems before. In limiting the choice of poems to those by contemporary authors, I wished to focus the inquiry on how these readers dealt with poetic text; I wished to avoid difficulties with reading that arise primarily from unfamiliar settings and the use of unfamiliar allusions, style, and diction. Canadian and British poems were used because another aim of this study (not reported here) was to consider whether the national origin of the poem influenced response in any noticeable way. For that reason, texts of the poems did not identify author[4] or national origin. The list of poems used is given in Appendix A.

Procedures

As stated earlier, the small-group procedures described here were designed to help develop in these adolescent readers a confidence in their own abilities as readers of poetry. The intention was to ensure that they would come to the Responding-Aloud Protocol (RAP) sessions ready to say what they were thinking as they attempted to make sense of a poem, that they would respond aloud with some degree of assurance that articulating their developing responses was not distinct from the effort to apprehend the poem.

Throughout this report I have used *responding, apprehending,* and *making sense* as though these terms were synonymous. I realize that these activities are inseparably part of a complex process; however, the invitation to readers in this study was an invitation to "make sense of the poem" or "arrive at an account of their experience of the poem" and in the process not to ignore the affective aspects of their responses. The phrasing cannot be more explicit without alerting the readers to specific kinds of end products. Both the small-group and RAP transcripts reveal that these readers interpret the terms loosely, that their focus is on making sense, which includes paraphrasing, reporting on the feelings and associations that the poem evokes, connecting with their own personal experiences, remarking occasionally on the language and form of the poem, and realizing from the poem what one might call a central significance.

Small-Group Discussions[5]

The class, in randomly constituted groups of five or six (except for the target group of six, which had been preselected to represent the middle of the middle-ability range) discussed one or more poems each day with the specific intention of arriving at an account of their experience of the poem. This account was shared with the class at the end of the discussion period. I found that six groups of five (assuming a class of thirty students) worked best.

4. I have since realized that omitting the authors' names might conceal from these readers the fact of the poems' constructedness, that there are people behind these poems. In subsequent studies I have provided the initials of the authors and explained that for the purposes of my research I did not wish the authors' reputation to exert an undue influence on the reading.

A typical fifty-minute period allows about ten minutes for getting started and closing, and about twenty-five minutes for reading and discussion. This leaves about fifteen minutes for the reporting-back phase, just about enough time for five reports and the clarifications and elaborations students usually seek and provide. The procedures for group discussion are demonstrated initially with the whole class by the teacher. The procedures are simple.

1. Groups are formed. Each group chooses a reporter, who will chair the session and report back to the large group in the plenary session. Members of the group take turns reporting from one day to the next.

2. Copies of the poem are distributed. The teacher reads the poem aloud.

3. A student reads the poem to the whole class. The teacher determines from the reading probable sources of misunderstanding caused by syntax or unfamiliar words. ·

4. The teacher invites inquiries about meanings of unfamiliar words and allusions, and assists without directing interpretation. Students are encouraged to respond to such inquiries, but this stage of dwelling on words even before the context has emerged is not drawn out.

5. Within each group, one member reads the poem aloud.

6. Within each group, each student *in turn* reports an initial reaction, feeling, or observation occasioned by the reading, including feelings of frustration or puzzlement. Members of the group do not remark on one another's responses until each member of the group has shared an initial response. **Note:** This is an important stage in the process and should be strictly followed. Students who do not expect to understand a poem by and for themselves, even after three or four readings, ought to realize that their initial responses often provide important clues as to how the poem speaks to them. Moreover, it is quite likely that these possibly important prompts will dissipate when an articulate member of the group provides a coherent and convincing account of the poem. In far too many classrooms such accounts convince uncertain readers that their own initial responses are irrelevant and misleading, so that they learn to shelve their responses and wait for the teacher to provide the cues that will lead them to the preferred reading.

This round of sharing initial responses eases the passage to further contributions, especially for reticent speakers. When and as these initial contributions are seen to matter in the developing discussion, they provide a necessary boost to the confidence of these students.

7. Following this preliminary round of comment, the students are no longer required to speak in turn and may comment freely on what they

5. I have added some details to my account in the earlier edition in the light of clarifications I have had to make during several demonstrations of the procedure and my own use of the procedure in a variety of classroom settings. The procedure in outline remains unchanged.

have just heard and share observations in their endeavor to arrive at some sense of the poem. A means of keeping the discussion going is to have the students read in turn a sentence or stanza at a time, commenting as they go along. This allows the students to interrupt with comments and questions as they build up their sense of the poem. It also helps the group to establish the text of the poem: what is and is not there in the text, particularly in light of the various impressions they have just heard. This part of the discussion is often driven by the need to prepare a report for the plenary session.

8. Any time an impasse is reached in discussion, the students are encouraged to return to the text of the poem.

9. Students are also encouraged to reread the poem in the light of the understandings that have emerged during the discussion.

10. About twenty minutes into the discussion, the teacher alerts the class that they have five minutes to prepare their reports. The members of the group take account of any meanings that have emerged and prepare an account that represents their experience of the poem, this account to be shared with the larger group. At all times, the teacher's concern is not to influence the form and content of this account. However, students are discouraged from taking written notes. This is an important feature of this procedure. Notes record where the group has been rather than where it has arrived. Reporters relying on notes settle too easily on what they have recorded and are not alert to possibilities of meaning arising from what other reporters say. At first, students feel insecure speaking without notes, but because other members of the group can prompt them, they soon function effectively without them. They also realize that, at least in poetry, one may but should not settle too early on meaning, and that their final reports are open to revision in the light of what other groups report. Since reporters are encouraged to build on what previous reporters have said, such a developing response will often shift from what the group may have settled on earlier. Moreover, as they hear other groups report, reporters recall, and place as relevant, aspects of the discussion that had not figured in their earlier versions.

The large-group session usually involves students reporting in turn for their groups, with the order of reporting shifting from day to day. After the first group has reported, the onus is on each subsequent reporter to build on the previous account, agreeing and disagreeing, and reporting any new insights that have occurred in the process. Initially, groups are happy to report first, quite sure that the last group to report will have little or nothing new to say. From about the fifth session on, the groups begin to value hearing other accounts of the poem, against which they can develop their own account. After each report, the teacher asks members of the group if they wish to supplement their reporter's account of the poem or to record minority opinions.

11. The several accounts of the poem should create the impression that the poem is much more than each of the summary accounts has made out. It remains for the teacher to raise questions that arise from the discussions and the groups' reports, to help relate some of the several strands in the groups' reports, to introduce where useful the terminology that helps the class make sense of and place their observations. During this summarizing, the teacher should at all costs avoid creating the impression that the groups do not have the resources within themselves to deal adequately with the poem and that the teacher is the ultimate repository of and arbiter of the poem's meaning. The questions that are raised by the teacher at this concluding stage must be real questions sparked by an interest in the inquiring of the students and reinforcing a belief in their own resources as readers.

When discussing this procedure with teachers, I have often been asked to elaborate on the role of the teacher. Teacher intervention in the group process is meant primarily to encourage the members of the group to pursue inquiry or reread the text with that intent. At no time does the teacher during small-group discussion volunteer an interpretation or suggest where one may be found. Exceptions, of course, must be made to prevent frustration and loss of interest. On the whole, the procedure is structured but, as far as can be helped, nondirective. I acknowledge that the structure itself invites a particular approach to the reading of poetry (it does invite, for instance, frequent rereading); however, I would argue that the approach does not in any way direct how meaning and what meaning is constructed from the text. If the group procedure influences the meaning-making process in any way, it does so by insisting on the participants' listening to one another and on their attending, via the frequent rereadings, to the text they have before them.

Readers who are concerned about the larger aims of teaching poetry may wonder whether these procedures, though they set worthwhile objectives, do not focus too narrowly on "making sense" at the expense of formal and aesthetic concerns. In fact, formal and aesthetic concerns arise in the discussions, but only in oblique ways. However, to push the discussion in those directions would be to introduce notions that these students (disaffected as far as the formal study of poetry is concerned) are not ready to address. I would add that once students have recovered their confidence in their ability to read poetry, formal and aesthetic awarenesses do enter the discussion, not explicitly but integrally tied in with talk of significance and meaning. The students I have in mind want above all to understand the poem, to realize or apprehend its meaning; they would be the first to recognize that such understanding goes beyond paraphrase. From what they have said in interviews and journal comments, many of them see no connection between their growing regard for poetry and past discussions of formal features such as rhyme schemes and figures of speech.

I admit that the invitation to "make sense of a poem" may convey to the students the impression that they must not attend primarily, say, to matters of form and diction or report on what feelings the poem evokes in them. In practice, however, the first round of students' comments in the small group is essentially an attempt to record first impressions, and these invariably include how the poem affects them. The following extract from a discussion by fifteen- and sixteen-year-olds of A. J. M. Smith's "The Lonely Land" is taken from the middle of the discussion and shows how even then the pupils will speak of how the poem affects them:

Jim: Well, what do you get . . . what do you . . . ?

Syl: I get loneliness.

Mike: This guy says emptiness.

Anne: I get like, loneliness . . . .

Syl: . . . and, like, innocence, like it hasn't been developed or anything . . . it hasn't been . . .

Jim: What do you get?

Pete: Sorta, like, eh . . . it's untouched.

Ray: It's sort of, um, being unwanted.

Jim: No.

Anne: Unwanted?

Ray: No, that's no . . .

Anne: What?

Syl: Lonely.

Anne: Loneliness.

Ray: Unwantedness. Darkness.

Syl: Darkness? How do you get that?

Ray: It's . . . the storm, when there's a storm, there's no sun and all that, you know it's . . .

Syl: It's got dark, lonely feelings.

John: But somehow I get . . .

In this segment, the repetitive, overlapping discussion touches on their experience of the poem as well as on how they understand the poem. If, during the discussions, the students attend to formal concerns, they do so because these aspects of the poem are highly salient and may provide a clue to how the poem should be read and understood. Thus one of the fourteen- to fifteen-year-old groups discussing Stevie Smith's "The Best Beast at the Fat-Stock Show at Earl's Court" notices the poet's instructions that the poem should be read in monosyllables and proceeds to do so in order to discover how such a reading might help understanding. Again, one of the reporters for the fifteen- to sixteen-year-old group sees how the text of Alden Nowlan's "The First Stirring of the Beasts" is arranged and comments:

> Well, um, the thing about the first stirring, like, after the second paragraph there's that little part . . . "unsure and a little afraid, / And after a little" . . . like, it's . . . it's . . . not part of the . . . the sentence; it's as if he falls asleep or something.

Overall, the discussants' focus remains largely on making sense. Such an end does not exclude their personal response to the poem: how they experience the poem, the experiences called up by the poem, the feelings that the poem evokes. Nor does a focus on making sense preclude their noticing the formal aspects of the poem or particular aspects of the poem's diction.

Although it is clear that the group discussion protocols provide valuable data on the responding process, it is important to remember that these discussions serve essentially to prepare students for the RAP sessions so that they may think aloud uninhibitedly and at length as they work their way toward meaning. An obvious problem with this study (and a likely explanation for the paucity of such work) lies in the difficulty and expense involved in obtaining accurate transcriptions of small-group talk and individual protocols. Large-scale sampling is usually out of the question. A case study approach with an emphasis on close analysis and "thick description" is a more feasible endeavor.

For several reasons, the small-group discussion needs to be undertaken as part of a whole-class activity rather than as an activity involving the target group isolated from the rest of the class. It is the target group's accountability to the other groups that drives its discussion and sustains its effort. All groups were tape-recorded even though only the target group in each class was actually being monitored. Such a procedure avoids singling out the individuals being studied; it also provides additional data to which one can turn for corroboration. I was also able to videotape the group being studied without drawing attention to them. These videotapes have proved valuable in transcribing and interpreting the small-group talk, where meaning is often modified by gesture and other non-vocal signals.

Daily Poetry Journals

Students were asked to keep a daily poetry-response journal during the small-group discussion phase. They were to set aside each evening enough time to reread the poem they had discussed that day and to write down their response: the feelings the poem evoked in them and their understanding of the poem, given that sufficient time had elapsed for them to have reconsidered and confirmed or questioned further their experience of the poem. They were reminded to comment on as many aspects of the poem as would account for and clarify their response. The journal writing was not intended merely as a source of additional data; I hoped to reinforce the notion that newer understandings can emerge with later rereadings and that, in the light of newer associations, the poem can continue to "grow." As Terry Eagleton (1983) puts it, one never reads the same poem twice. I responded to the journal entries in ways that indicated I had read them with interest and valued the contributions.

Stream-of-Consciousness Reports

A few days after the RAP sessions (see the next section), the two classes were asked to read a poem and jot down whatever occurred to them as they read through the poem and afterwards. They were encouraged to repeat the procedure through several readings of the poem, each time clarifying and developing their response to the poem. Two thirty-five-minute sessions were scheduled. The poems used were Sylvia Plath's "Mushrooms" and Margaret Atwood's "Dreams of the Animals." An account of such a procedure is found in an article by Sharon Silkey and Alan Purves: "What Happens When We Read a Poem" (1973).[6]

Collection of the RAPs

At the conclusion of the group discussion sessions—twelve in all—students involved in the study recorded their responses to two poems in two separate private sessions, a few days apart. The interviewer turned on the tape recorder and instructed each student as follows (this statement, however, was not read verbatim to the student):

> As you know, we are trying to understand how people go about making sense of a poem. Today you and I are going to read this poem. I want you to tell me what you think and feel as you try to understand this poem. First, I'll read the poem aloud and you can follow in your copy. After I have read the poem, tell me what your feelings and thoughts were as you heard the poem, and what they are immediately after. Feel free to ask me about any words you aren't sure of. You can then read the poem silently or aloud, telling me your thoughts and feelings as you read and after you read. You can read the poem and comment as you go along as many times as it takes you to make sense of it. You may stop whenever you feel you have nothing left to say, at which time, you or I might read the poem again to pick up any ideas and impressions that just then might occur to you.
>
> Once again: I would like you to keep in touch with the way you are understanding this poem and the way that understanding changes and grows. Tell me anything that goes through your mind as you read the poem. *Everything* that you're thinking is important; don't leave anything out just because you think it might not be relevant. If I say anything, it will be to answer your questions or to remind you to say what you're thinking.

6. Both the journal entries and stream-of-consciousness accounts together with the group discussion protocols are intended to supplement the RAP protocols and other data as comprehensive case-study files are compiled on each of the twelve students. In this study, they served primarily to corroborate my reading of the protocols.

Remember: any kind of response, reaction, thought, or feeling. Do you understand?

RAPs and Context

The RAP-collecting procedure creates a particular reading situation that should be taken into consideration when assessing what occurs during the process. I recognize that all utterances are "contextually-bound" (McHoul 1978, 117), that any reading situation, as ethnographic research has made so clear, is bound up in a complex of attitudes, expectations, and social and psychological concerns (see, for instance, Green and Bloome 1983; Gumperz 1982; Kantor, Kirby, and Goetz 1981; McDermott 1977).

In the RAP-collecting procedure the interviewer is explicitly a listener who, throughout the small-group discussion phase, has announced an interest in the processes by which the reader makes sense of and responds to a poem, has disavowed any concern for one right meaning, and has demonstrated an openness to possibilities of meaning and a conviction that adolescent readers can read, respond to, and make sense of a poem for themselves. Such a stance, it is hoped, will help counter to some extent any tendency on the part of readers to anticipate what the interviewer wants them to say or to meet any school-derived expectations of what one says when one talks about a poem. The situation directs only that readers make an effort to make sense of the poem, attend to their responses, and think aloud while they do so.

Of course, the in-school setting (with all the constraints that it implies) is inescapable; and interviewers, however nondirective, cannot easily mask their teacherly role. Even the most careful interviewer may involuntarily encourage some responses more than others. Moreover, the interviewer's initial reading of the poem itself offers an interpretation. Such concerns can be met to some extent by forgoing the initial reading by the interviewer and by dropping the role of interviewer altogether and having readers tape their RAPs in private.

On the other hand, for the kind of students I have worked with, the role of the interviewer as partner in keeping the conversation going is worth retaining. And though the interviewer's initial reading may influence the students' interpretations, I believe this situation is no different from the ones they face in their classrooms and that the RAPs will, to an extent, be representative of their efforts to make sense in such contexts. Also, on the basis of the RAPs I have received, I am inclined to discount the effects of that first reading on the larger patterns of reading revealed by the RAPs.

How readers conceive the task of reading and responding to a poem will determine to a large extent the content of the RAPs and will be for the researcher a primary question that directs how the RAPs must be read. The interviewer's main concern during the RAP-collecting procedure should be to ensure as far as possible that the situation does not constrain or direct the reading of the poem (Mishler 1986).

Analysis of Protocols

Protocol analysis has generally proceeded along the lines of dividing the protocols into units and then tracking the process in terms of those units. These units range variously from phrases, clauses, T-units, and sentences to statements, propositions, and episodes. I chose to proceed differently.

"A true content analysis," says Cooper, "eschews a priori categories of any kind" (1971, 21). My procedure was one of generating constructs from the data and then bringing in additional data to test the reliability of the constructs. I believe it is the data that must reveal the categories by which response to poetry may be analyzed or charted. These categories must be grounded in the data, and not be, as with many studies of response, imposed on the data from outside. This is not to say the analytical schemes already established were not considered; however, the data and my own questions suggested that such schemes might not be entirely appropriate.

Personal Background Interviews

Anticipating that I might need to assemble comprehensive case study files on each of the twelve students, I administered a personal background questionnaire in order to obtain information, among other things, on the students' reading habits, interests, attitudes to poetry, and self-perceptions of themselves as readers of poetry. These interviews were conducted immediately or soon after the RAPs were obtained, so that their perception of themselves as readers often took account of the process they had just gone through. As with most of the other supplementary data, the information gleaned from these interviews does not figure in any significant way in the account of the results in Chapter Three. That account relies primarily on the data provided by the RAPs.

3

Results and Data

In reporting the results of the procedures described in Chapter Two, I am very much aware that the data I have worked from are far too voluminous and dispersed to be offered for easy reference. Each of the small-group discussions that could be transcribed is about twenty-eight double-spaced manuscript pages long. Fortunately, the small-group work is not the subject of this report, and, though it deserves study in itself, I have limited myself to reporting on it only in terms of its place in the design of this study, that is, as preparation for obtaining the Responding-Aloud Protocols (RAPS).

The RAPs are on average seven double-spaced manuscript pages long. Four sample protocols with commentary are presented in Chapter Four. In addition, Appendix B contains four complete, uncommented protocols so that readers themselves can test out my analyses on original data. However, as I explain later, the RAPs are only the visible tip of a complex organic process. They are to be read as a whole, and there are few, if any, separable segments to point to in support of my understanding of the reading patterns they represent. Where I can in my discussions, I provide illustrations from the RAPs.

RAPs and the Place of Small-Group Discussion

Several concerns directed my attempt to track the reading processes of the twelve students I had identified for this study. Chief among these was a concern to ensure that the responses I obtained would be fairly representative of the processes by which these students went about making sense of poetry. Furthermore, I wished to be sure that they would come to the responding-aloud interviews with a sure sense of their own ability to make sense of poetry and to articulate their responses uninhibited by anticipation of what I wished to hear or by prescriptions carried over from past classroom encounters with poetry.

My experience confirmed the expectations I had built on the process of undirected small-group discussion. From my observations during the twelve days of group discussion and my examination of the transcripts of these discussions and of the daily journal entries, I became aware of several developments. First, the procedure helps develop articulateness in talking about poetry and boosts students' confidence in their own resources as readers of poetry. Moreover, because the teacher's role is as far as possible nondirective, the procedure encourages independent thinking and risktaking in formulating statements about the poems. This is particularly noticeable in the cases of shy and less articulate members of the group, who appear to discover that they can make valuable contributions to the work of the group. Finally, there is a gradual movement away from defensiveness about one's opinions and an intolerance of others' opinions toward tentatively holding and confirming or revising personal opinion by attending to the text and the opinions of the group. This is most easily recognized in the increasing use of words and phrases like *perhaps, could it be that, maybe,* and *I wonder.* At the same time, one notices a decreased willingness to adopt easily the opinions of the most articulate or dominant member of the group and an increased willingness on the part of the latter to consider the opinions of other group members.

Several aspects of the small-group discussion procedure are particularly effective in assisting such developments.

Sharing Initial Responses

Having each member of the group, after the initial readings, mention in turn an initial response (an observation or statement of feelings aroused by the poem, or even *like, dislike, don't understand, am puzzled*) allows for placing on the table responses that probably would be shelved and forgotten if not immediately articulated. If such a step is not allowed for, it is quite likely that one person in the group will say something that will convince the others to set aside their own responses as being "inferior" and not particularly pertinent. Also, the diversity of responses initially presented allows group members to realize that the poem they have before them may not be so obviously what each of them thinks it is.

Second, what is offered as an initial top-of-the-head response does not have to be immediately justified. It is in every sense a provisional reaction, allowing group members to change their minds and contradict themselves later. It certainly encourages a collaborative attitude and a tentative stance.

Third, not being able to articulate one's initial response can be inwardly disruptive because one may then hear something else that is quite plausible, which is immediately taken up by the group. Some notions nag at the mind and are hard to dislodge. If articulated, such notions might be seen immediately as a misreading or as demanding a rereading of the text, or they might be picked up by the group for consideration. If the less articulate members of the group, particularly, are not given the opportunity to voice their initial reactions, they may come to believe that what they think is likely to be unrelated to what is being discussed. If they have announced their initial reaction, and if it does in some way bear on the discussion, they will know that they have a stake in the outcome of that discussion.

Reporting Back

Reporting back to the large group at the end of the twenty-minute small-group session ensures in general that the small group will work assiduously toward arriving at some statement about their sense of the poem. They are fully aware of their responsibility to the class as a whole, and are anxious to hear what the others have to say, particularly because they must in their reports take account of what the previous reporters have said. Through the ten days of such discussion, it became apparent that the groups came to understand that their own contributions were not the final word but an important part of a truly collaborative process.

The Reporters

Given the number of small-group sessions, each member of the group will act as reporter for the group at least twice. It is interesting to observe how the group reporter takes on the role of chair, drawing from the group a statement that best represents their sense of the poem. As one of four or five reporters to the large group, he or she must take account of what previous reporters have said (except when reporting first). It was not unusual for members of the group to fill in when a reporter was in need of assistance or had missed reporting a vital point from the group's discussion. Most reporters, in the journals they kept daily during the project, expressed self-satisfied surprise at how well they had represented their group, particularly because they had spoken at length without notes. At the same time, it was clear to the members of the class that each report could provide only the gist of the preceding discussion and fell far short of representing the complete discussion.

I must stress again that, in terms of the methodology of this study, the small-group discussion process is intended to ensure that pupils will come to the individual RAP sessions with some confidence that they can read a poem and say what they are thinking as and after they read it several times in their effort toward meaning. They will know that what they feel and think does matter, and that articulating these thoughts and feelings, however irrelevant they may seem at the moment, is an important step toward making sense of the poem. The experience in the group confirms for some as well that seemingly irrelevant "flashes" can at times turn out to be keys to the poem's meanings.

The Responding-Aloud Protocols

The RAP-collecting procedure was successful much beyond the modest expectations I had set for it. I had intended that the first run of RAPs would be a preparation for the second run of RAPs, which would then provide the actual data for the study. It turned out that the first set of RAPs met all my hopes that the students would think aloud as they tried to make sense of the poem and that they would speak at length and with little hesitation. Thus the size of a crucial database had doubled. It was clear, as I heard them speak and later listened to the tapes, that the students were working not from any expectations as to what they must say, but from a desire to arrive at understanding. The presence of a tape recorder was less inhibiting than one might have expected, quite likely because over the twelve days of small-group work the students had become used to the presence not only of tape recorders but also a video camera and a prowling photographer as well.

The protocol transcripts, on average seven double-spaced pages long, include interruptions from the interviewer, these interruptions being mostly in the way of urging the students to express their thoughts and asking occasionally for elaboration (see Appendix B). The transcripts represent from fifteen to thirty minutes of the students' thinking aloud as they attempt to make sense of the poem. They do not indicate the reflectiveness of the speaking, although pauses are indicated. Twenty-six RAP protocols in all were obtained from twelve students in the target group and two other students whose contributions during the small-group sessions had been sufficiently interesting to warrant including them in the RAP sessions. Two of the protocols were poorly recorded and could not be transcribed.

I should point out that the subjects for the RAPs were interviewed in two separate private sessions, that they had come to know the three interviewers during the small-group work sessions, and that none of the interviewers were in any position to influence their school grades. It is quite clear, as one glances through the verbatim transcripts of the RAPs in Appendix B, that the interviewers did not maintain a scrupulously nondirective stance throughout the RAP interviews. In fact, the interviewers *thought* they had until they reviewed the transcripts and discovered otherwise. Fortunately, with one exception, few if any of the interviewers' inadvertently directive remarks or prompts (e.g., "good!") were of sufficient consequence to warrant my withdrawing any particular RAP from the data to be studied.[1]

The RAPs record a process, a reader's attempt to make sense of a poem through several readings. I do not claim that the RAPs represent the process fully nor that the process recorded is a complete account. Admittedly, much of that process is unconscious and tacit, probably inaccessible to conscious

1. In their transcribed form, reminders from the interviewer to students to speak their thoughts may sound far more insistent than they were in context. It was often apparent in the interview itself that a student was so involved in reflecting or puzzling over a particular aspect of the poem that he or she would forget to think out aloud.

probing, and likely to remain unarticulated or, at best, merely hinted at in the spoken account. Again, the RAPs provide a record of initial (but concerted) encounters with poetic text; they do not provide data on what occurs later, when the poem is recalled and reflected on, and when it engages a network of associations and meanings that includes other poems as well. I have come to realize that these initial encounters are powerful determiners of how the poem will continue to be read, a point I return to later in this report.

It may be argued that the RAP procedure invites what Rosenblatt (1978) would call an efferent reading of the poem ("the primary concern of the reader is with what he will carry away from the reading," p. 24), that the aesthetic, lived-through experience of the text is ruled out in the process. Be that as it may, an examination of the protocols reveals that they provide a much fuller account of the initial encounter between adolescent reader and poem than, as far as I am aware, any other means available to research. Whether we like it or not, it is initial encounters that most classroom teaching of poetry attempts to deal with, and it is these crucial first efforts that the RAPs, I believe, document and help us to understand. The RAPs should tell us, for instance, how seemingly erratic interpretations emerge and become established in the mind of the reader or what preliminary groundwork precedes seemingly fortuitous recognitions.

The RAPs also tell us how individuals differ in the ways they go about making sense of poetry. It became clear as I studied these transcripts that each pair of protocols presented a distinctively individual pattern of response; and as I became more familiar with the protocols, clearly identifiable markers emerged to confirm their distinctiveness. There was some difficulty, though, in sorting and setting out these markers in order to establish these individual patterns. This is a complex, organic process made up of specific moves by the reader and influenced by, for instance, the expectations the reader brings to the poem, the reader's attitudes to poetic text, and how the reader conceives a reader's responsibilities. Factors that determine how a text is read, such as a reader's attitudes, expectations, and world knowledge, are perceived not in isolation from other elements that influence how the text is read, but in the context of a continuing interactive relationship between them and the text. In the discussion of my findings, these factors are isolated for analysis only to demonstrate that what is perceived as an individual pattern of reading turns out to be so on analysis as well.

I am describing, in short, the process by which I myself realized that there were distinctively individual patterns of reading and then sought identifiable criteria that could be applied to the protocols to confirm the existence of these patterns. I report these results in four parts. The first part, which follows in this chapter, provides a sampling of the data: the texts, interspersed with commentary, of four RAPs on Seamus Heaney's "Blackberry-Picking." These sample RAPs offer readers an opportunity to consider what patterns of reading are represented in the larger sample. My commentary on these readings is informed by a familiarity with other supporting data, not least of which are these readers' voices on tape and their other RAPs. These four texts exemplify the four patterns of reading I describe in Chapter Four. That chapter is in three parts. The first part describes the elements in the process of reading that have helped me to track the four patterns of reading and to account for the differences among these patterns. The second part describes the four major patterns of reading that I identified from my study of the RAPs, and which are represented in the four sample protocols. The third part considers the interrelation among these patterns and the elements that compose them.

Four Readings of Seamus Heaney's "Blackberry-Picking"

Blackberry-Picking

Late August, given heavy rain and sun
For a full week, the blackberries would ripen.
At first, just one, a glossy purple clot
Among others, red, green, hard as a knot.
You ate that first one and its flesh was sweet   5
Like thickened wine: summer's blood was in it
Leaving stains upon the tongue and lust for
Picking. Then red ones inked up and that hunger
Sent us out with milk-cans, pea-tins, jam-pots
Where briars scratched and wet grass bleached our boots.   10
Round hayfields, cornfields and potato-drills
We trekked and picked until the cans were full,
Until the tinkling bottom had been covered
With green ones, and on top big dark blobs burned
Like a plate of eyes. Our hands were peppered   15
With thorn pricks, our palms sticky as Bluebeard's.

We hoarded the fresh berries in the byre.
But when the bath was filled we found a fur,
A rat-grey fungus, glutting on our cache.
The juice was stinking too. Once off the bush   20
The fruit fermented, the sweet flesh would turn sour.
I always felt like crying. It wasn't fair
That all the lovely canfuls smelt of rot.
Each year I hoped they'd keep, knew they would not.

In this poem the speaker recalls childhood experiences of picking blackberries, being caught up in the desire to collect a large amount, the sad realization that the berries would not keep, and the recognition that the process would be repeated each year. The poem is narrative in structure and mode; the causal and temporal interrelations among the events are clearly laid down. On the surface, at least, the reader is not called on to make more than the simplest inferences to determine what happened. But the reader also must come to terms with an imagery that suggests that the poem is dealing with much more than a mere greed for blackberries.

It seems that not only simple greed but uncontrollable desire is the subject of the poem. The appeal to the senses—taste, touch, and sight—and the references to flesh, blood, and Bluebeard, and the children's brooking no obstacles to collect more blackberries, all suggest a greed and a lust out of control. The aftermath of such unrestrained desire is presented in images of decay and rot. Yet each year the children proceed in the hope they can have it all and not pay the price. I do not wish to present the poem as a simple morality tale; there is a rich ambiguity about it that a summary cannot capture. I suggest an interpretation only to point out the possibilities available to readers.

The RAPs that follow are meant to demonstrate, first, that the research procedures I have described provide rich data on the initial encounters between adolescent readers and poetic text, and second, that there are easily recognizable differences in the ways adolescent readers go about making sense of poetry. These RAPs—the second set for the four readers—were selected because they clearly demonstrate differences in patterns of reading, which can be discerned as well in the first set of RAPs from the same readers given in Appendix B.´

Though it may appear so, my account of these readings is not tailored to support the description of the different patterns of reading. I have transcribed most of the text as spoken, summarizing only where this could be done without misrepresenting the substance of the response.[2]

Angie

Angie is a friendly fourteen-year-old who, at the time of this study, had read very little poetry. Her recreational reading is limited to mysteries and fiction about teenagers. Her grades are generally around the class mean. Born in Canada, she is the daughter of first-generation East European immigrants and is under some pressure to do well in school. She plans to go to secretarial school after completing high school.

The interviewer reads the poem and not receiving an immediate response, he asks Angie whether there are any words she does not know. Angie goes through the poem picking out words whose meaning she is unsure of. She asks in turn about *briars, trekked, clot, byre,* and *fermented.* The interviewer pro-

---

2. (unclear) indicates indecipherable speech. Pauses of different durations are represented as follows: . . . (less than five seconds); *pause, long pause, v. long pause* (five seconds to one minute). It was during the longer pauses that the interviewer would remind readers to say what they were thinking.

vides the meanings. One wonders why Angie does not attempt to derive the meanings from their context and whether her requests are just a ploy to gain time. The interviewer asks whether she has any initial reaction, and she responds,

> (*laughs*) These people like blueberries, I guess, 'cause they're . . . they're picking them and picking them. I mean they just notice that you can't . . . hold them very long without them rotting . . . or . . . oh (*laughs*) I don't know . . .

Angie's stance of uncertainty and lack of confidence seem unwarranted. She appears to have made out the plain sense of the poem and noted two controlling ideas: that these individuals seem driven to pick as many berries as they can and that they cannot keep them long without their spoiling. As she appears reluctant to say more, the interviewer invites her to read the poem silently and comment as she goes along. Following a long pause, she asks what "A rat-grey fungus, glutting on our cache" means. She is offered meanings of *fungus*, *glutting*, and *cache*. After a very long pause, she says,

> Well, so it's about, like, how they pick the . . . these blueberries off every season, how they're different and stuff, like, at the beginning . . . when they were ripening, like at first they were just little . . . just clumps of . . . blue or whatever, like little blueberry things.

It is clear from her initial response that Angie has an idea of what is happening in the poem; however, her making sense of the poem seems to be directed entirely by an intention to provide a literal account of what the poem is about. In order to prevent any misreading that might be caused by her miscuing on *blackberries*, the interviewer explains what they are. Angie continues her hesitant account:

> First, like, they were red . . . like, that's when they were just ripening, and they were, like, sweet, you know? It's like a thickening wine, like they have to take time to ripen to be good, you know? If it's—(*pause*) And the summer's blood was in it, like, that's just when it was ripe. Like it was made from, you know, the summer and all this. And . . . but, like, they really liked now this 'cause . . . they ate it a lot and they just kept picking and picking and . . . then after a while they liked it so much that they went out with more milk-cans, pea-tins, like . . . they went more, with more and more things to get more bushels of it.

It seems as though Angie sees her task as one of literally translating text. Her heavy use of *like* reveals her uncertainty about this task and, together with *you know*, is an appeal to the interviewer for confirmation. (Only a few occurrences of *like* have been edited out of subsequent quotations.) Her paraphrase continues:

> And it didn't matter, like, if they got scratched by the thorns or what-not; they just wanted some more. And . . . they seemed to rot very fast because,

while they're picking it the ones at the bottom are already starting to . . . turn green and all this when the ones on top are nice and you know, dark and black. (*long pause*) I guess they try so much to have as many as they want, like they put it in these big baths . . . but they notice that they can't keep it, 'cause it just gets rot . . . more rotten and rotten. And like it says, "Once off the bush / The fruit fermented" Like, it would . . . it was very good, like, once you picked it you could eat, but once if you held it more and more, it would get more rotten . . . and they would turn sour.

(*long pause*) And then . . . you know, they were all sad, like . . . it's such a waste that they have all these things but it would just keep rotting on them. And I guess they'd do it . . . "Each year I hoped they'd keep" I mean, they would like, I guess . . . like, during the winter they'd like to keep it and what-not, like, just save it up but they can't because it just keeps rotting on them, like it's not meant to be held. It's just, you know, meant to be picked and then eaten right away.

(*v. long pause*) But it was this late August (*pause*), I guess that's what makes (*unclear*)

Well, I guess that was the last time they could ever have these blueberries 'cause in the winter they . . . I guess they couldn't grow.

(*v. long pause*) I guess it's just about the . . . blackberry picking, like . . . it's just how they pick it, how they try to save it and have more for themselves, but . . . it just can't be. That's it.

With "That's it," Angie announces she has completed her account of the poem; there is nothing more to be said. The paraphrase stays with the basic narrative and causal sequence of the events in the poem. There are inferences to be made but none that are required by the simple narrative she has created: "how they pick it, how they try to save it and have more for themselves, but it just can't be." Thus she does not venture outside the literal sense of the text to acknowledge that she has felt the effects of the images of lust, hunger, and decay. Her "it's not meant to be held" seems promising; and her concluding, "but it just can't be" is indicative of her having sensed the gap between the children's innocent hopes and their grasp of the inevitability of decay. But elaborating on that sense does not seem to be in Angie's remit as a reader of poetry, a remit exemplified by her "I guess it's just about the blackberry picking."

As one reads her account, one becomes aware how much it is contained by and dwells on the two impressions she gleaned from the initial reading: "they're picking them and picking them" and "you can't hold them very long without them rotting." Little that does not pertain directly to these two impressions is brought in, and if it is, it is misread to conform to the "they won't keep long" notion. Thus, "Until the tinkling bottom had been covered / With green ones" becomes in her paraphrase, "while they're picking it the ones at the bottom are already starting to turn green." She ignores the allusion to Bluebeard and does not pause to wonder about "burned / Like a plate of eyes." "Late

August" suggests fall and the onset of winter; so she is able to ascribe the disappointment of children to their not having been able to preserve the blackberries for the winter. Thus the excess is understandable. The "lust for picking" has become a concern to preserve. So the theme of the poem, as we see in the next extract, is somehow reduced to the generalization that you cannot take something away from its surroundings and expect it to keep.

The interviewer invites Angie to read the poem again, this time aloud. This reading appears to bring no new insights, only a reconfirmation of "the facts":

> I guess, like, you know, you can't take something away from its surroundings and try to keep it and keep it 'cause it'll just . . . like, get sick and it'll just rot, you know. That's about it. (*v. long pause*) And they're just saying how good the first ones were, until after, like the rest they couldn't eat, you know . . . 'cause they would be rotten. (*long pause*) And they tried so hard, like they, they . . . they got scratched from the . . . thorns and everything and they, they wanted more and they had big cans and they put it into vats and they tried keeping it but it could just never be. That's about it.

The repetition of "That's about it" points to Angie's anxiety to close. It is quite likely that she believes she has done what she can and thus her last contribution is in the form of a concluding summation fleshed out with a few supporting details. In an effort to tap a dominant impression, the interviewer asks if the poem leaves her with "any sort of feeling." She responds,

> Well, you can't take something away from what it is . . . without it . . . turning upon you I guess.

It is interesting that Angie has not let *her* feelings, *her* experience of the poem, intrude (at least overtly) into her account and therefore once again she provides a moral. The interviewer presses her to say what feelings the poem evokes in her. Her response is to try to explain the disappointment felt by the individuals in the poem ("You just get more and more depressed and you just feel like crying"). The interviewer persists: "And is that how this makes you feel?" She responds,

> In a way, yes. Yes. Well, I feel sorry for the people that are doing so much work and . . . it all just turns back on them and rots. That's it.

Once more she has announced closure. So the interviewer asks whether the poem is just about blackberry-picking (as she had said earlier) or whether she thinks it is about other things as well. She responds,

> Well, it's mostly about blackberry picking. I guess, they just put it as an example. 'Cause the poem is about blackberry picking, it's just . . . could be just, like, an example to show that you can't take something away from its, you know, surroundings. But the poem is about berries. (*pause*) And about the people picking the berries, mostly.

Angie appears to be bound by her initial hypothesis. She might be willing to go further, to reexamine the poem, to question her initial response, to consider the feelings the poem might have evoked in her. But her reading in light of the limited objectives she appears to have set for herself has left no questions in her mind that would necessitate such reconsideration. It is no wonder then that, when the interviewer asks if there is anything she would like to add, any observations, confusions, or other thoughts, she says there is not:

> (*v. long pause*)I don't think so. (*v. long pause*) No. That's about it. Like, it's just how they just go around picking it and . . . trying to save it . . . which rots on them. That's about it.

This is the fifth time in her protocol that Angie has announced "That's about it." She is not being uncooperative. Having found a satisfactory account of the poem, she has settled on it and is unable to see how a closer look or an alternative hypothesis is worth considering. She is not unlike some other readers in being unable to shake off initial impressions, particularly when such impressions seem to fit the information derived from the text.

Pierre

Pierre is an affable, shy fifteen-year-old, fluently bilingual (his father is English-speaking, his mother is French). He is the eldest of three children. He says he reads about four books a year, mostly adventure and detective fiction. He had read little poetry before the study and generally dislikes it. His favorite school subjects are history and mathematics; he excels in the latter. Overall, his grades are slightly above the class average. After the interviewer reads the poem, Pierre inquires about the meaning of two words, *briars* and *trekked*. When these words are explained and he is invited to share his initial impressions, he hesitantly offers, "like, sort of like a . . . a family? like and . . . and newborn babies, and stuff."

One is tempted to suggest that Pierre does not censor stray thoughts and associations, or one can assume that Pierre is honest in reporting his initial impressions of the poem and that these are not necessarily unconsidered reflections. Pierre is obviously reporting initial impressions; he does not feel the need to explain or clarify this response, and I am not sure that he can. It remains to be seen whether these initial responses direct subsequent readings in any way as they did Angie's readings. He is invited to read the poem and does so aloud. He inquires about the meaning of *cache* and *byre*.

Reminded that he must say what he is thinking, he responds that he finds this difficult because he cannot "really pick up what's happening". It seems as though Pierre expects to sense meaning. Much of the process by which this might happen remains unarticulated simply because Pierre's typical stance is to ponder silently, waiting for meaning to emerge. He decides to reread the poem and asks whether he should provide a literal account of the poem, by which he most likely means a paraphrase. Taken with what he has just said, this question is revealing. It suggests that Pierre sees his task primarily as one of formulating meaning, that he sees the poem as having a meaning below its literal surface, and that he thinks his task is to mine this meaning. I do not think Pierre believes that a literal paraphrase would be particularly useful; he probably suggests the procedure because he has gotten used to doing it during the small-group discussion phase, where it was essentially a means of establishing the text, of "placing the text on the table," so to speak.

In his paraphrase he comments on the ripening process, how the berries "get sweeter as the sun gets to them." He notes how the children lusted for the berries and worked hard to get them. He is silent for a while; it turns out he is wondering why they would pick the green ones. He goes on,

> So I guess when going through the bushes . . . all prickly . . . sort of pricked up their hands.
>
> (v. long pause) So I guess they picked too many berries here and . . . when they store them, after a while, like . . . I don't know . . . they picked too many so . . . some of them go bad 'cause they've been . . . you know, in the byre too long . . . But every year, I guess, the person gets carried away and keeps picking them and picking them . . . hoping that they'll keep, they'll stay . . . good for a while but . . . always knows . . . that they're not going to keep. I guess that's 'cause he just gets carried away and goes, like—(pause) It's pretty hard down here.

This extract, punctuated as it is by *I guess* and *I don't know*, reveals an uncertainty about meaning that is belied by the adequacy of the paraphrasing. Pierre's attention is not on the surface meaning of the text but on the poem's deeper meaning. It is for this reason that he searches for the point of what is being related. When he says, "It's pretty hard down here," it turns out it is because he cannot grasp what is really happening in the poem. His uncertainty about the poem and his confusion about what he is expected to do as a reader are not unrelated and emerge in the inarticulateness (and indistinctness) of his response to the interviewer's question, "What's hard?":

> It's hard to figure out (*pause*) 'cause usually there's (*unclear*) like . . . don't know . . . (*unclear*) . . . puts you on the track of something else but—

It is clear that Pierre cannot find anything in the poem to get him "on the track of something else," something other, we can surmise, than the plain sense. He is invited to reread the poem in the hope this will help him, and he does so silently. He is reminded to stop at appropriate moments in his reading to comment on the poem and to identify any aspects of the poem that puzzle him.

Pierre comments as he reads silently; however, this account is just as hesitant as his earlier account. Again he paraphrases, pausing frequently and long. He asks what is meant by "the red ones inked up" and later what *hunger* means in "hunger / Sent us out." He cannot really understand "dark blobs burned / Like a plate of eyes" but is given no help by the interviewer on that one. It is not surprising that Pierre in this his fourth run through the text must inquire about some additional phrases whose meaning he is not sure about. On the one hand, as a move, it substitutes for the thinking aloud he is urged to do while he reads; on the other hand, because his attention is so much directed by what may lie below the surface meaning of the text, he may not have recognized some features of the text he has yet to make out. In any case, he provides us with another paraphrase of the text, this time dwelling more on the latter section, which deals with the discovery that the blackberries have spoiled. He concludes,

> They looked so nice on the bush and that, and when you picked them right off the bush they were nice and juicy. But after . . . you take 'em off the bush and then, so you store them and then . . . they don't . . . they're not as good as . . . when they just came off the tree.

By this fourth reading Pierre has established for himself what the text is literally saying but expresses some uncertainty about what it means; however, the understanding that the blackberries are not as good as they were when they just came off the bush is the clue to the meaning that he has been groping for all along. After a very long pause, he continues,

> Somehow I get these feelings, eh . . . it doesn't make sense though. A mother there, having kids . . . and the first child is always . . . I guess nice. It says here . . . "a glossy purple clot." Always, the first child's always . . . the nice . . . it's fun to get the first child, I guess, and then . . . it's interesting and then . . . once you get into it you can't stop and then soon . . .
>
>   . . . when you say lust, I'm thinking maybe lust for children? Maybe you like the chi—love children? But then, I guess, maybe . . . children . . . some are better than others, like some are . . . like the green ones aren't as nice or they're not as bad. Some of them are nicer, at least after you've had so many that . . . you start to look a little different? I haven't much experience in (*unclear*) but . . . that's all I get now.

Pierre's concluding remark, "that's all I get now," is quite telling. Meaning is something one gets; however, Pierre is unsure about his interpretation as he attempts to apply what he gets to the poem. He warns, "Somehow I get these feelings, eh . . . it doesn't make sense though." Pierre doesn't trust that his interpretation will make sense to anyone else simply because he is unable to account for how he arrives at this meaning. While Pierre appears to believe that he has just arrived at this meaning, it is clear that his initial impression, "sort of like a . . . a family? like, and . . . newborn babies, and stuff," has imperceptibly directed his reading of the poem and finally been elaborated in this account of parental disillusionment. He is now able to read the poem in a way that confirms his theme.

Because meaning is something you get from a poem, Pierre does not find it necessary to return to the text to test out this meaning. Instead, when asked if he has any further impressions or final comments to make, he abandons the text and launches into generalities such as, "There's a great amount of truth in this," and "It's a nice poem, I guess, whenever nature is . . . there's always a certain amount of beauty in it." His concluding remarks reveal that he is not fully satisfied with his interpretation of the poem: "I wish I could get some . . . a little better, you know, like . . . I'm not . . . too satisfied with what I have here" and "I always wish I could get more out of it though."

It is hardly surprising that Pierre is not satisfied with his interpretation of this poem. He reads the poem in the hope of getting meaning. To that end he takes several but seemingly unrelated stabs at meaning ("this means that" or "I get this"), hit-or-miss affairs that often seem to frustrate rather than help. Prior knowledge is seldom brought to the text in a deliberate way as part of a strategy to assist in interpretation. Thus Pierre's relating the meaning of the poem to family relationships, "newborn babies, and stuff," in the early part of his protocol is not a deliberate strategy; he himself cannot account for the association. Because the text of "Blackberry-Picking" is narrative in form, Pierre has no difficulty realizing the context in which the poem is set, and his protocol is not as discontinuous as his protocol on "Cyclops," a poem that is non-narrative in form (see Appendix B). In that protocol we become aware of a series of uncoordinated attempts to mine the poem for meaning, attempts to realize the context and the meanings as well. But despite the unity provided by the narrative of "Blackberry-Picking," we become aware through Pierre's hesitations, his verbalizations of I don't know and I guess, and his occasional remarks like "It's hard to figure out," that Pierre is actively searching for meaning behind the plain sense of the narrative.

Petra

Of the four readers, Petra is the only one who admits to reading poetry on her own. She is fifteen years old, the second of three children, and speaks and writes English and French fluently. She is quite involved in outdoor sports, and her favorite reading (about one book per month) is in that area. She would like to be a flight attendant. Petra can be described as quiet but friendly. Her grades are generally slightly above the class mean. She seems relaxed during the RAP interview and talks quite freely.

After the interviewer has read the poem and Petra has been told the meaning of three words she is unsure of, she speaks about the mood the poem creates. She speaks of a feeling that comes in August that summer will soon pass and winter is coming. The ripening blackberries bring out the feeling of summer, and the hoarding of the blackberries suggests the onset of winter: "Snow is going to come and everything is about to go away." After she has reread the poem silently, she confirms that "it's the same thing that I said first." She elaborates on the feelings underlying the realization that the berries had rotted:

> They found . . . whoever is the author found . . . fungus on the . . . they
> would go through heck trying to pick it and, you know, get all . . . you know,

it was worth it, all sticky and everything. And then to find that they all rotted and everything. It's really, you know . . . it's really . . . sad; it wasn't fair.

Urged to continue thinking aloud, she responds: "I don't know . . . I guess
that's about it for the general view." While "it wasn't fair" appears to be a
direct quote from the text, it is more likely at the same time an expression of
Petra's own response. Moreover, it sums up her sense of the poem's meaning,
the "general view," as she puts it. It remains to be seen whether this "general
view" is reapplied to the poem so that the poem is reread as an elaboration of
that view. In her RAP on "Cyclops," whose mode is non-narrative, Petra when
invited to reread the poem, launches immediately into an account in which the
elements of the poem are realigned and interpreted to fit a generalization
about human behavior. Interestingly, because of the narrative features of
"Blackberry-Picking," the reader is not called on to infer a great deal in order
to determine the situational context or the plain sense. Because the narrative
exerts a certain control over the reading, it is less likely that the reader will
find gaps that need to be filled in and explained, as in Petra's reading of
"Cyclops," by an elaboration of the general view or impression created by the
poem at first reading.

Invited to comment on the poem line by line or wherever she feels it necessary to stop and comment, Petra begins to paraphrase the poem. Unlike
some other readers, she does not paraphrase to find out what the poem is saying. Instead, she is guided by a clear sense of what the poem is about, the
"general view" that she has already established. Implicit in her account is a
view of life as unfair: winter was coming, the children were driven to pick the
berries (the attractiveness of the berries and the desire to provide for the winter contributed), and as they picked, their hunger grew, brooking no obstacles
and causing them to put up with some pain to get what they wanted. But when
they had filled the bath with all the canfuls they had collected, Petra says,

> They found a . . . fungus all over it, you know, and they said, "Oh my God,
> you know, we did all this for nothing." . . . It wasn't fair . . . He was hop-
> ing, you know, every year, okay, they have to keep, but he, you know, deep
> down inside he knew they'd rot away . . . before he ate them all.

Her paraphrase, guided as it is by her "general view," ignores aspects of the
text she is unable to comprehend or fit into her notion of the disappointment
and unfairness of it all. Thus she is arrested by the image, "on top big dark
blobs burned / Like a plate of eyes," considers a likely meaning, is unable to
make sense of it, and sets the difficulty aside to continue her paraphrase. She
runs immediately into, "Our hands were peppered / With thorn pricks, our
palms sticky as Bluebeard's." Her response is,

> Okay, I guess that explains it. They went through, you know, . . . thorns,
> they're probably very . . . full of . . . [she likely wishes to say *blood* but
> doesn't], they went through that just . . . to get what they wanted.

It isn't that other students recognized the full force of the allusion to Bluebeard; it is just that Petra is now reading the poem primarily to expand on her earlier statement of what the poem is about, and both blobs burning like a plate of eyes and Bluebeard are passed over without notice simply because she has already made sense of the poem and those elements she cannot yet accommodate will eventually fall into place. With Petra's strong "impression" of the meaning of the poem or, to put it another way, her sense of the contours of the poem, she is unlikely to formulate a general statement that strays any distance from or is not in accord with the larger meanings of the poem. A general statement allows her to withdraw into further generality to accommodate otherwise intractable elements in the poem, or to bypass them entirely.

Petra concludes her paraphrase with,

> At first, you know, you're . . . so enthusiastic even though you know they're going to rot away, you'll still go out there and . . . almost break your back trying to find, you know? I guess spending days . . . picking blackberries . . . before the winter came and then storing it and then finding they all rotted away . . . pretty awful feelings.

Her use of *you* is indicative of her intention to generalize. Even though the particularities of the blackberries and their rotting away are retained, the poem, for Petra, is an expression of the disappointment that follows when enthusiastic and difficult effort is wasted—"pretty awful feelings," as she puts it.

Petra is reading, as I say later, like an allegorizer; that is, as a reader who attempts to find a close parallel between the events in the poem and events in real life. Unlike Angie, she goes beyond paraphrase. Unlike Pierre, she is not reading the poem searching for meaning; instead she has a sense of the meaning of the poem (a statement about Life) and reads the poem with the intention of finding the markers that illustrate that statement. In the case of "Blackberry-Picking," the narrative so directly bears out the statement about Life she has established for it that her task turns out to be little more than reiterating the instances of desire, effort, and the bitter aftermath. Her propensity for allegorizing is more clearly illustrated in her "Cyclops" protocol, where the non-narrative mode of the poem requires her to infer not only a statement about Life but also its metaphorical components in the poem (that is, what in life is represented by this and that element in the poem). In general, poems that call for a great deal of inferencing are more likely to bring out the allegorizer in a reader like Petra.

David

David, fifteen years old, is regarded by his teachers as someone who ranks potentially among the top 20 percent of his class academically. His favorite subject is history. He admits to not being interested in poetry and believes that most of his English teachers find what he has to say about literature irrelevant and distracting. After the interviewer has read the poem, David inquires about *byre*, *cache*, and *Bluebeard*. Soon after explanations have been provided, he announces,

> Right away I get the thought, I could see it's really well done, the way they
> . . . explain how it tastes and everything. Summer's full out and all this . . .
> "glossy purple clot," "sweet / Like thickened wine." I can almost taste it.
> Really good and . . . "milk cans, pea-tins, jam-pots." That reminds me . . .
> sometimes . . . when my family used to go . . . blackberry and strawberry
> picking and we had . . . all that stuff.

David is open to the experience of the poem. He relishes the images, which immediately call up past experiences of berry-picking. He inquires about *potato-drills*, and when told the meaning, he decides that at least for now "there's not much to say." He's invited to read the poem silently or aloud as he wishes.

After a long pause, and pausing as he reflects aloud, he begins to probe beyond the literal sense of the text. As he says, he is "trying to compare it to something . . . in life . . . ." He believes there might be something in the notion of separation, decay, and death implied by the taking away of the berries from the plant and their spoiling. He notices, as he glances through the poem, the line, "But when the bath was filled" and inquires what a bath has to do with this poem; he is given an explanation that does not go very far. Unlike with most members of the group, nothing seems to escape David's attention—it is just possible that *bath* may provide a clue to the underlying significance he is searching for.

As he reads lines 3–7, he remarks,

> Now that's . . . It sounds . . . just . . . I could almost feel . . . a raspberry on
> my tongue . . . It's so . . . explicit. Very descriptive.

David's protocol reveals very clearly how the experience of the poem is not filtered out in the thinking-aloud process. What is more important to note, however, is that David attends to his feelings, his sensations as he reads the poem. As he continues to read, he notices the image, "Like a plate of eyes," pauses, and then continues reading, making out the plain sense as he goes along. He wonders why "anyone would pick green ones," assuring the inter-viewer (who unfortunately volunteered that the green ones might have been collected accidentally) that he had had a summer job picking berries and had never picked green ones. He returns to "and on top big dark blobs burned / Like a plate of eyes":

> I don't know how they compare that . . . to be . . . all . . . in a mass. More
> like flesh. *(laughs)* *(long pause)* You poke it, it bleeds.

David is not rushing to make sense of the poem and therefore is quite pre-pared to articulate those associations thrown up by his reading. He misses the full force of the Bluebeard allusion because, like many others in the group, he confuses Bluebeard with Blackbeard the pirate:

> "palms sticky" I think that . . . to do with Bluebeard was, was . . . because . . . a part, that he was a part of it, a part . . . he wanted a . . . as much . . . treasure as possible. See, he . . . tried to grab it (*unclear*) sticky hands.

At least an aspect of the basic sense of the image has been retained—there are protocols where readers who are aware of or have asked about and been told Bluebeard's history, begin to realize that *lust* may have far wider connotations. He asks for and is told the meaning of *glutted*. After a long pause, scanning the text and mumbling to himself, he reads lines 20–24 and remarks,

> This person . . . seems young. "I always felt like crying." Most people don't cry over . . . berries. (*laughs*)

One notices in David's protocols the constant reference to experience. Most readers of this poem operate on the assumption that the speaker is young; few appear to be aware of the fact that they are drawing such an inference. After a long pause during which he appears to be rereading the text, David says,

> I get the feeling that . . . the berries are like . . . innocent. Like . . . take the innocence away from . . . whatever is guarding it . . . and you take it away and then . . . something's going to . . . destroy it, like, not destroy but . . . take advantage—devour—that's . . . fungus. Taken away from . . . its mother, the plant, put in a bathtub and then it's . . . I don't know, how can I put it? ah (*laughs*) killed by a . . . fungus. (*laughs*) (*v. long pause*) Fermented. Actually, I wouldn't cry about that—could make some wine.
>
> [The flesh?] would turn sour. (*long pause*) "all the lovely canfuls smelt of rot." (*long pause*) I guess the person hopes that . . . well, maybe . . . I get the feeling that in a way she felt (*pause*) she was . . . (*long pause*) doing wrong or something. 'Cause all these things going to waste. (*pause*) "I always felt like crying." What a waste, all this.
>
> (*softly*) There's not very much to talk about here. It's not like the other one ["Cyclops"].

David has returned to and expanded on a hypothesis he advanced earlier—he senses an innocence under attack by a destructive fungus and the speaker's sense of having done something wrong. He speaks, as he did earlier, of getting a feeling. At this stage he cannot provide an explanation, and hence we hear there's not very much to talk about. The interviewer urges him to take another run through the poem.

This time David, with some notion of what is happening in the poem, takes a closer look at the text. He assumes that the season, late August, probably "signifies something." It is autumn, animals shed their coats (he reminds himself that they breed in the spring, not fall), everything ripens. He tries to make something of "thickened wine," considers a meaning of "tasting life" but thinks it's more like "blackberries being tasted by" life. After all, "summer's blood" was in them. As David reads, he is open to several associations that spring up; he even sets them up:

> Let's see . . . if I was a blackberry . . . "Leaving stains upon the tongue" (*pause*) being murdered (*laughs*) "and lust for / Picking" (*unclear*) Get them!

He explores the meaning of "Then red ones inked up," then notices, "There're all sorts of hard consonants: *bleached, boots, hayfields, cornfields, potato-drills, trekked.*" He's not unaware of the technical aspects of poetry; however, he considers them not for their own sake but for what they might tell him about the meaning of the poem. As he says of this last effort, "Don't know about that." He is not sure what he can make of it.

As we proceed through David's protocol, we become increasingly aware of his tentative stance, of his awareness of the possibilities of meaning:

> "Until the tinkling bottom" empty, I guess . . . you could see that there's emptiness . . . until it's totally covered. (*pause*) "on top big dark blobs burned / Like a plate of eyes." That I'm not sure about. That's puzzling. "burned" Why would they burn (*unclear*) like eyes; a plate of eyes. (*v. long pause*) I get a picture of a plate of eyes, all these eyes on a plate; "big dark blobs burned / Like a plate of eyes" (*v. long pause*) I can't get that.

David, not for lack of trying, is unable to find the link between these images and the tentative structure of meaning he holds in his mind. He questions information in the poem that does not conform to what he knows, his world knowledge. So, as he reads lines 17–19, he says,

> I don't understand why . . . right away . . . like just when they hoarded the berries . . . 'cause I, I . . . fungus doesn't usually come right away. It takes awhile, doesn't it?

He realizes, as he goes on, that they must have collected a large quantity and recognizes the force of *hoarded*. He even wonders whether it isn't the moisture that makes things rot.

> As soon as I hear "bath," I hear . . . I get this feeling of moisture, water. (*long pause*) Why a bath? Why not big pots? or wooden crates? or bowls?

Here again is evidence of David's respect for the integrity of the text. (Or should one say, this is an instance of his "privileging" the text?) The text may be saying something that he might just miss. Could the bath have contributed to the spoiling of the berries? And does it matter if it had? He sets the question aside to attend to "rat-grey fungus" and "glutting on our cache." Again he speaks of the strong feelings these images evoke, and yet his account of the poem thus far seems to him inadequate to the force of these images:

> It seems . . . well, I . . . I get the feeling that there's a . . . a meaning behind it, not just the literal meaning; but it's . . . it's hard to get, it's hard to grasp. Most poems—just about every single poem has a . . . something behind the

> literal meaning. (*long pause*) This one . . . I have the feeling that there's
> something else . . . but I can't . . . quite grasp it.

David is not anxious to close; he trusts the poem and he trusts his own
response. He feels strongly that there is more here than his account thus far
has recognized or accommodated. So he makes another effort:

> It's a . . . a season where everything is ripe . . . so all these people . . . get
> together . . . Okay, well first . . . I get this picture . . . more, something like
> a story; possibly a girl, who's walking through the forest, she sees some
> blackberries. She tries one, it tastes really good. She goes home, gets a
> whole bunch of friends . . . and their family. They go picking, they pick all—
> they go all over the place, every little nook and cranny picking all these
> things, they have so many of them. Like here: "Our hands were peppered /
> With thorn pricks." I mean, that doesn't . . . after, you know, like half hour
> after . . . a long, long time.

David is creating a scenario in the hope that meaning will emerge. If I may
use James Moffett's paradigm (1968), David hopes as he relates "what is happening," he will realize "what happened" and eventually, "what happens." His
last few phrases reveal the difficulty of the underlying effort: what is strongly
sensed and yet hard to grasp, to make sense of. He goes on, and interestingly,
though he has not been interrupted or distracted, shifts into the past tense,
"what happened."

> Our palms were sticky. Like they were squeezing . . . they got juice all over
> their hands. And they hoarded . . . they . . . that's a lot, they got a whole
> bunch of them . . . in their barn; then they found out after the . . . that their
> . . . container . . . the bath was filled . . . that . . . it was . . . being infested
> with fungus. So the . . . girl felt bad. Then she . . . kept wishing that . . . the
> . . . they would . . . ah . . . this fungus wouldn't . . . develop. (*v. long pause*)

In quoting David here, I retained more of the pauses than I have been doing
thus far. I wished to indicate that he is involved in a process of consolidating
what has emerged from his readings. It is a more selective narrative; yet it falls
short of interpreting, of moving toward "what happens." He pauses long
enough to cause the interviewer to urge him to speak on, to say what he thinks
it might mean. David seems to pick up where he left off:

> (*long pause*) Well, "fungus," like . . . and "rat-grey," I associate that . . . evil
> (*unclear*) Something . . . that I . . . some . . . people; funguses, basically not
> that different if you look from the blackberry's point of view. I mean . . .
> something huge and they can't do anything about it unless they're . . . still
> on . . . their, the plant. What you get is these people picked them; and they're
> all going . . . stale. (*v. long pause*)

In considering what it might mean, David returns to an initial, [but it seems]
persistent response: the vulnerability of the berries once they are off the bush.
He pauses longer this time: somehow a meaning, a significance, consonant

with the strong feeling he is aware of, evades him. The interviewer suggests he read the last section of the poem aloud (in pointing to a particular section of the poem, this intervention is far more directive than it seems at first glance). David reads lines 17–24 aloud.

> In the first stanza they . . . they give this feeling, beautiful blackberries and then . . . then here, they're ugly. Right away they seem ugly. They're attacked by the fungus. And . . . I don't see any, ah . . . words that . . . make . . . nice words . . . except one, "sweet": "the sweet flesh would turn sour." [Interviewer: Oh you mean in the last stanza there are—aren't any nice words.] It's all ugly, or stinking, fermented, all . . . dull feelings. (*long pause*) (*laughs*) and . . . we can't do anything.

It is significant that, after he has read the last section, David returns to the poem as a whole to note the difference in the way the blackberries are described. He is working at accommodating his observations into a meaningful account of the whole poem. Responding to the interviewer's quizzical look, he jokes that those "dull feelings" may be explained by the fact that the speaker is a girl ("Girls!"), and then wonders why he gets the feeling the speaker is a girl. (One wonders whether David feels the description of the spoiled blackberries displays an excess of queasiness —something he considers more in keeping with the sensibility of a young girl than a boy.)

As the tape appears to be running out, the interviewer inquires if there is anything David would like to say about his feelings or thoughts or "the meaning of it."

> Gives me this . . .warm, the first thing gives me a warm feeling. I could actually taste it just when I read it, really . . . very good and . . . I understand how . . . like, you know this crave, they're going all over the place looking for berries. I've experienced that myself. Then . . . until, you know, they had so many that their hands were all sticky . . . and finally when they get a whole bunch . . . they . . . they didn't take a bit at a time. That's it, that's it, that's the reason behind it. I got it, I . . . I can get it. Take a little at a time, you'll be able to build up . . . and . . . if you eat a little at a time . . . won't go stale. But if you take a whole bunch, it'll spoil. Like, don't take too much. Like . . . if you buy too much of something . . . either you'll get sick of it or it'll go stale.

One can forgive David for the moralizing; all stories (and most poems), he has learned, point a moral; one would, however, be wrong in assuming that all along David had been searching for a maxim or a lesson. He had announced earlier that the poem had a meaning "in life"; he had related what "had happened," but the generalizing "what happens" appeared to evade his grasp. His final summation begins by taking us through his experience of the poem, confirming what we have already heard. It appears as though his phrasing, "they didn't take a bit at a time," triggers a recognition of the consequences of excess. His excited recognition, "That's it, that's the reason behind it, I got it,

I . . . I can get it," points out how much David is aware of his own comprehending, what reading research refers to as metacognitive awareness. (Such
evidence is present throughout the RAP.) We can be sure that David is aware
of the inadequacy of his trite formulation of the poem's meaning and that the
strong images he had recognized require a much fuller formulation. It isn't
surprising that despite his seemingly triumphant realization, he announces
almost disappointedly, "There's got to be something else."

The interviewer commends him for his effort and suggests he take the
poem home and read it over. David's response to the interviewer's reassur-
ances would delight any reader-response critic: "I feel like, you know, I made
the poem."

In several runs through the poem, using a variety of strategies, David has
indeed made that poem. Readers will have recognized several strategies and
what one might call stances, but the ones that stand out are his constant refer-
ral to his own experience, his consideration of a variety of hypotheses, an
openness to possibilities of meaning, his respect for the integrity of the text,
and a willing attendance to his own sensibility—summed up best in his oft-
repeated, "I get the feeling that—"

These four RAPs are not exceptional in the extent to which they justify the
account of the patterns of reading I present in Chapter Four. The second set
of RAPs from the same readers is just as clearly exemplary (see Appendix B).
RAPs from other readers in the study can with little difficulty be assigned to
one or another of the four patterns, though some RAPs are more problematical than others. Above all, these accounts more than adequately support my
claim that RAPs provide rich data on the initial encounters between adolescent readers and poetic texts.

4

Findings

Elements in the Process

To isolate and identify the elements in a complex process is to somehow reduce and denature them. The elements described in this chapter exist and must be understood in the context of a reader's relationship with the text. They have no existence in and of themselves. As Rosenblatt (1985, 100–101) puts it, arguing against a mechanistic, linear approach to studying the responding process,

> We have to think of them [elements], not as separate entities, but as aspects or phases of a dynamic process, in which all elements take on their character as part of the organically-interrelated situation. Instead of thinking of reading as a linear process, we have to think rather of a complex network or circuit of interrelationships, with reciprocal interplay.

The descriptions that follow must be read with that caveat in mind. The elements I describe are to be viewed as interrelated and interactive so that, as the reader's understanding shifts and moves, even slightly, consonant shifts and moves probably register elsewhere in the process.

The list of elements that follows is drawn from several fields: literary critical theory, reader response criticism, theory and research, discourse theory, reading theory and research, and cognitive psychology (e.g., Richards 1929; Squire 1964; Goodman 1967; Purves with Rippere 1968; Smith 1978; Rosenblatt 1978; Spiro, Bruce, and Brewer 1980; Brown 1980; Culler 1981; Brown and Yule 1983). A rather lengthy initial list covering a broad spectrum of responses was pared down to just those elements likely to figure in the protocols of our adolescent readers. As these elements were applied to the protocols, the list was further reduced and clearer definitions emerged. Because the focus was on tracking a process, on identifying "readerly" behavior rather

49

than on itemizing elements that constitute the process, the list describes attitudes and actions rather than the features of a written or a spoken product. Thus the elements listed here are unlikely to appear as the obvious characteristics of discrete portions of the RAP texts; rather, they must be inferred after several readings, and in most cases, only as the larger outlines of a pattern of response have begun to emerge.

For all these reasons, the elements are best understood as some of the poles between which the readers in this study range. Plotting lines along the points between these poles would not only provide outlines of patterns of reading a poem but would also help identify and account for the differences in these patterns. I say "some of the poles" because I do not wish to claim that the elements I have listed represent *all* the attitudes, expectations, and behaviors that a reader of poetry may reveal in a protocol. The elements fall into two major categories: what the reader brings to the poem, and how the reader moves through the text of the poem.

It bears repeating that these categories and their respective elements have been specified primarily in order to identify the nature of and account for the apparent differences among the RAPs. The elements are closely interrelated and interactive, not in a linear, mechanical sequence but, to repeat Rosenblatt's insistence, in an organic way:

> "Expectations" and "experiences" which the reader brings are not entities
> for interaction, but stances or states of the organism, as are linguistic activities. (1985, 101)

It will be apparent as we proceed that this list of elements is specific to the process of reading a poem. I should also make it clear that I am not arguing that these elements point to conscious or deliberate choices on the reader's part.

What the Reader Brings to the Poem

Literary text immediately sets up expectations, especially within school settings. The mere fact that they are reading a poem will cause readers to act in certain pre-set ways; certain expectations will have come to the fore so that readers pay attention to the text in certain ways. The reader's knowledge of literary conventions is certainly at work as well.

What does it mean to read a work as literature? What expectations are brought to literary text that are not brought to nonliterary text? A reader's expectations of how a poem means, how a poem must be read, and the kind of reality a poem represents powerfully direct the reader's intentions and actions. Not all or even most expectations and intentions are as salient features of the protocols as this list might make out. They must be inferred from several readings of each protocol. An underlying expectation that governs all our readers is the expectation that the poem can be returned to for rereading and that portions of the text can be quickly accessed for easy reference.

A Reader's Expectations of How a Poem Means

Readers of literature expect that literary text is meaningful. Culler (1975) suggests that readers of literature adopt "a rule of significance," that is, they assume that the writer will attempt to say something significant about the human condition. It follows from that assumption, as Dillon points out, that readers of literature "generally want to be able to say something insightful or at least clever about what they have read" (1980, 168).

In this study, the small-group discussion sessions sought to ensure that the students would come to the individual RAP sessions with a confidence in their own ability to make sense of poetry. The expectation that a poem will make sense (that is, reveal some significance) to concerted individual inquiry is apparent to one degree or another in all the protocols. Its most evident manifestation is the *absence* of an attitude that a poem does not make sense unless its exploration is mediated by the teacher, primarily by means of questions. The willingness to undertake the task and the confidence that meaning will be arrived at are present in varying degrees; so is an implicit belief that talking about a poem with an interested and uncritical listener cannot but be helpful. Thus one may take risks in articulating meaning and not be called to judgment. This expectation operates in all the protocols I studied; I believe, though, that such an expectation would not have operated as consistently if the students had not been prepared in the way they were. This element is therefore defined essentially by an absence of such behavior as constantly turning to the interviewer to ask, "What do I do next?" The readers in these protocols pause, some more frequently than others, but they appear to know full well that they must and can work out the meaning of the poem for themselves.

We can also assume that these readers do not expect a poem to make immediate sense (even though some teacher questioning behavior may have created that expectation).[1] None of the RAPs read as though the students expected to have understood the poem at first or second reading; there is an unmistakable tentativeness about their early formulations of meaning. It is the expectation that the text will make sense that allows readers of poetry to remain, as Harste and Carey (1979) put it, "cognitively active." Such an expectation allows them to go beyond the inferences that are accessible to most readers to those inferences that demand considerable effort and a fuller awareness of the possibilities of meaning. When readers in most classroom encounters with poetry announce that a poem does not make sense, they are most likely announcing that they cannot infer the complex interrelationships that make the poem meaningful, that is, the configurations within which the elements in a poem make most sense.

1. I have in mind those classroom situations (fortunately declining in number) in which teachers, after one or more readings of a poem, proceed to ask questions seemingly with the full expectation that students will have ready answers. If the expected answers are not forthcoming, the teacher usually provides them.

While all the readers in this study operated as though a poem would make sense, their expectations as to *how* a poem makes sense made a considerable difference to their readings.

1.1 A poem is a complex way of saying something simple.[2]   With this expectation, the reader's task appears to be to penetrate the text and structure of the poem to arrive at a meaning that is usually a generalization about life or nature or the like. Usually, after the first or second reading, the reader announces a rather general theme for the poem and then proceeds to read the text in a superficial way to support that theme. Thus Angie announces, "I guess it's just about the . . . blackberry picking, like . . . it's just how they pick it, how they try to save it and have more for themselves, but . . . it just can't be." Such an approach becomes apparent when a reader ignores those aspects of the text that do not fit too easily into the theme he or she has announced. Other readers with such an expectation keep searching for the key that will unlock the puzzle. Pierre is one such reader.

1.2 All aspects of a poem contribute to the meaning of a poem and must be taken into account in one's reading.   Unlike readers in 1.1, readers whose expectations fall into the present category do not gloss over puzzling aspects of the poem. They often set such portions of the text aside until they believe they can deal adequately with it or must confess failure. For such readers, whatever is written in a poem and how it is written matter. The difference among readers is the degree of mattering; some are more willing than others to work at fitting in intractable elements in the poem and to achieve some degree of congruence.

Story-recall experiments reveal that the memory is selective in what specific information in text is recalled (Spiro 1980). Such selective recall may not apply to the same degree for readers of short poems who may have become conditioned to consider all elements in the text significant, some more important—for primary consideration—than others. For example, normally, establishing the setting or the role and identity of the speaker may take precedence over noting features of rhyme; however, unusual features of form may also be taken up immediately. Interestingly, the title was not an element in the text that featured prominently in the RAPs unless there was some dissonance between it and the contents of the poem. Even then, it was noticed only on subsequent readings.

The expectation that they can quickly reread the poem may lead readers to establish sets of priorities that determine what should be attended to first and what may be set aside for later attention. Thus David, early in his RAP, wonders about storing blackberries in a bath, sets the question aside, and returns to it later when he wonders whether dampness may have caused the mold to grow. I am not saying, though, that these are conscious, deliberate

---

2. The section numbers 1.1 and following correspond to the category numbers in Table 1, toward the end of this chapter.

choices on the reader's part; they are rather habits of mind, ways of looking. It is always important to remember in the discussion that follows that the poem is not only read but experienced as well, or as Rosenblatt (1978) puts it in a related sense, the poem is "evoked."[3]

A Reader's Expectations of What a Poem Means

The reading of a poem is influenced as well by readers' beliefs about the kinds of meaning that poetry represents.

2.1 A poem usually symbolizes or represents one of several stock themes about life or nature. Such an expectation is a counterpart of 1.1 and is easily recognized in the protocols of readers who approach a poem as though its primary function were to illustrate generalizations about life, nature, human beings, animals, and the like. These stock themes are applied like templates to the poem; that is, the poem is read to fit the theme, and aspects of the poem that cannot be accommodated are generally set aside or ignored. The degree to which the reader is able or willing to elaborate on such stock themes may help distinguish one such reader from another. Petra elaborates on the stock theme she identifies in "Cyclops," and Angie with the same poem is unable to go beyond a vague notion of animals "trying to give their impression of hunters or something like . . . trying to . . . act so big."

2.2 A poem embodies a complex meaning that is never fully realized but can grow with each reading. This expectation complements 1.2 and is most apparent in a greater concern for the integrity of the text, a willingness to return to those aspects of the text that cannot be fitted into the interpretation that is being considered. Another instance of such an expectation is a refusal to settle early on the meaning of the poem, to delay closure (see 4.9). Such an expectation is clearly evident in David's "Blackberry-Picking" RAP: "There's got to be something else."

Prior World Knowledge

What the reader brings to the poem is not only a set of expectations about poems and poetry but also a knowledge of the world that, depending on the poem and the reader, may be adequate or inadequate, appropriate or inappropriate. Rumelhart, who proposed the notion of story grammars to explain story comprehension, argues that even the simplest story comprehension task calls on a startling amount of information (1984, 20). According to Rosenblatt, "reading draws on the whole person's past transactions with the environment" (1982, 273). That environment would include past transactions with literary text and whatever knowledge of literary conventions the reader has acquired. World knowledge figures to some extent in every one of the RAPs, if only in that some readers reveal inadequate and often inappropriate

3. Readers' approaches to poetic text are obviously influenced as well by their beliefs about how they should proceed in making sense of a poem. As these expectations are revealed in the reader's moves (see 4.1–4.9), they have not been assigned a separate category in the list of elements.

conceptions of certain words like *hoard* or *lust* and their fuller connotations. Often there is sufficient redundancy in the text to fill in gaps or correct misinterpretations.

Spiro believes that "the relative contribution of prior knowledge will vary as a function of characteristics of the material being read, the purpose of reading, and the differences between individuals in their processing styles" (1980, 323). It is seldom that readers articulate what knowledge they are drawing on in making sense of a poem, though a failure to comprehend may be related directly to an inadequate conception of the reality referred to by the poem, an application of inappropriate schemata or knowledge structures. In "Blackberry-Picking," one such instance is the expectation set up for Canadian readers by "late August," the expectation that winter is coming. As typical Canadian readers, both Angie and Petra associate the blackberry picking with the need to conserve for the winter, and thus the "lust for picking" takes on more positive connotations and the consequent spoiling evokes considerable sympathy. Readers who do not relate the "lust for picking" with the need to preserve for the winter are far more likely to see the poem as an instance of uncontrollable desire. It is in this sense that students' cultural backgrounds, the sets of beliefs, assumptions, and attitudes that operate in one's daily living, are certainly part of one's world knowledge.

World knowledge, as such, is not an element that will easily help to identify particular patterns of response, though Spiro (1980, 324) suggests that it may be a distinguishing aspect of a reader's processing style:

> The extent to which knowledge structures are utilized in text understanding may be influenced by characteristics of an individual's text processing style. It may be the case that some readers tend to display relatively more processing resources towards fitting information in text with prior knowledge, while other readers prefer analysis of text as more self-contained units.

There are instances in the protocols where readers explicitly draw on world knowledge to make sense of the poem; or where associations, appropriate or inappropriate, are called up.

3.1 The reader is open to personal experience.   Often the reading will call up associations that may be either relevant or irrelevant (for instance, mnemonic irrelevancies, to use I. A. Richards' [1929] term for the latter). Such associations, more often than not, strongly influence the interpretation of the poem. In most cases, such experiences are difficult to set aside once the links have been established. Sometimes, the reader may deliberately draw on personal experience to elaborate on or test the validity of an interpretation. Again, the experience drawn on may be helpful or unhelpful.

3.2 The reader does not draw on personal experience.   This kind of reader does not appear to consider personal experience relevant in making sense of poetry. Most likely, the reader sees poetry as somewhat removed from life, in the same way as he or she sees much of the content of school subjects. For such a reader, poetic text is autonomous and needs to be understood on its own terms. Angie, for instance, reads "Blackberry-Picking" as though somehow its meaning resides entirely in the text. Thus, when urged by the interviewer to talk about the feelings the poem evokes in her, she states her feelings but sees no relation between how she feels and how she understands the poem: "Well, it's mostly about blackberry-picking" and "about the people picking the berries, mostly."

How the Reader Moves Through the Poem

What the reader brings to the text influences considerably how the poem is read, that is, the choice of strategies the reader employs. All readers in the study appeared to see their task as one of connecting, of filling in gaps, of resolving tension or conflict; that is, bringing together several strands of meaning in an effort to weave a single thread or make a text coherent. In that effort they may be faithful to the text or ignore the text when it appears to be intractable in the face of the meaning they are creating. Information may be altered or imported or ignored in this process. Thus the protocols display varying degrees of interplay between readers and texts. I use the word *moves* to convey the dynamic nature of the process; the reader is an active collaborator with the text in the creation of meaning. The moves listed in this section describe a variety of reading behaviors, some that complement one another and others that do not. Several terms used in the descriptions are defined as they come up: *bottom-up processing*, *top-down processing*, *frames*, *impressions*, and *hypothesis*.

4.1 Bottom-up processing of text.   Bottom-up processing in this context refers to working out the meaning of text by building up a composite meaning from the sentence or word level. It differs from top-down processing, which works out the meaning by assuming a context and predicting on the basis of the sentences already read (Brown and Yule 1983, 234). Most reading includes a combination of both activities.

I have in mind here a reader interpreting the text by focusing *primarily* at the local sentence level in the belief, most likely, that meaning in poetry derives mainly from attending to local meanings. The initial reading has failed to generate a directing frame that might guide further reading. According to Spiro, "The most obvious cause of an overreliance on the text in comprehension is the absence of relevant knowledge structures to utilize in top down processing—if schemata do not exist they cannot be used" (1979, 118). In the reading of poetry, schemata are not that directly available. The identification of what is an appropriate schema is in itself a large step toward meaning.

4.2 Frame-directed bottom-up processing of text.   I use *frame* strictly in the sense defined in Minsky's frame-theory: "a remembered framework to be adapted to fit reality by changing details as necessary" (Brown and Yule 1983,

238). I use the term *impression* in the sense of an indefinite or even sharp image or feeling that directs our understanding of the text. For this item I have in mind an approach to the text where attention is at the local sentence level but is directed by an impression or frame developed from the initial reading or expectation. In Angie's "Blackberry-Picking" RAP, we have an initial response ("These people like blueberries" and "you can't hold them very long without them rotting") that directs her elaboration of the text.

4.3 Top-down processing of text directed by a strong initial impression. The initial reading generates a strong impression or theme that directs subsequent readings of the poem. The impression or theme is sufficiently flexible to accommodate seeming inconsistencies. Such readers appear to trust their initial impressions or feelings as providing vital clues to a poem's meaning. Spiro (1982, 79) demonstrates, using an extract from Joyce's "The Sisters," that feeling can contribute independently to understanding, that a grasp of what the situation is about is not a necessary prelude to understanding.

An instance of such reading is offered by Petra's "Blackberry-Picking" RAP: Her initial impression is dominated by a sadness at the passage of summer and the longing to hold on to summer. The sense of unfairness at the rotting of the berries combined with this feeling of sadness dominates her rereadings of the poem, so that at the end she says,

> At first, you know, you're . . . so enthusiastic even though you know they're going to rot away, you'll still go out there and . . . almost break your back trying to find, you know? I guess spending days . . . picking blackberries . . . before the winter came and then storing it and then finding they all rotted away . . . pretty awful feelings.

4.4 Top-down processing of text—tentative frame. The reader proceeds through the text open to several possibilities of meaning. Unlike the reader described in 4.3, the reader does not settle immediately for the one frame or impression that will guide the reading. Such a stance is most apparent in both of David's RAPs.

4.5 Hypothesis formation—single. The reader proposes a single hypothesis to interpret the text. Such a hypothesis emerges usually after two or three runs through the poem. I use the term *hypothesis* in the sense of an expectation or explanation tentatively held, to be tested and set aside, modified, or confirmed as the text is read and reread. Rumelhart speaks of a "configuration of hypotheses (schemata) which offer a coherent account for various aspects of the text" (1984, 4). I prefer to use the term *hypothesis* to represent such a configuration or explanation.

On the face of it, there may be some question about the distinction between tentative frame (4.4) and hypothesis formation (4.5). Whereas a frame is imposed on the poem as a setting that might accommodate the poem's several details, hypothesis formation is the activity of construing a frame, a scenario, or an explanation from some of the details of the text in order to account for those and other details. In Pierre's "Blackberry-Picking" RAP, we are offered such a hypothesis toward the end of the RAP; however, the hypothesis is not really tested in another run through the poem.

4.6 Hypothesis formation—multiple.   In several runs through the poem the reader formulates hypotheses to take account of newer realizations. There is a difference here between readers who consider in turn and reject several hypotheses and those who consider and hold tentatively several hypotheses until a satisfactory account of the text begins to emerge. Pierre's reading of "Cyclops" provides a good example of the former; David's of the latter.

4.7 Drawing on personal experience.   Some readers are more likely than others to turn to personal experience to help interpret the poem or to elaborate on an aspect of its meaning. Personal experience includes reading experiences as well. This move is related to the element described in 3.1 and 3.2 and is included in this listing because it figures as a strategy in the protocols of some readers. Both Petra's and David's RAPs provide instances of drawing on personal experience; in David's case, his is a deliberate strategy: "I don't understand why . . . right away . . . like just when they hoarded the berries . . . 'cause I, I . . . fungus doesn't usually come right away. It takes a while, doesn't it?"

As I have already pointed out, some readers appear to take the information provided by the text as an unquestionable given.

4.8 Early closure.   Consonant with some of the preceding moves is a desire to terminate discussion or close. Alternative readings are not attempted or even considered as a possibly worthwhile move. Neither does there appear to be a felt need to confirm the validity of one's reading by another run through the text. Angie illustrates such a stance: having set limited goals for herself as a reader of poetry, she is anxious to close and announces quite early, "That's it."

4.9 Delayed closure.   There are also readers who are not anxious to close, who feel there are yet gaps in their accounts of the poem, who are puzzled by aspects of the poem they have yet to work out. At the same time, these readers recognize that a fuller understanding is not beyond their grasp and that given time and possibilities of exchange with other readers, they might work out a more complete reading. Clearly, David delays closure because he has yet to accommodate aspects of the poem that do not fit within the hypotheses he is considering.

The Reader's Relationship to Poetic Text

As we become familiar with the protocols, we become aware that readers perceive the role of the text and their relationship with the text in very different ways.

5.1 The reader attends closely to the text.   The reader regards the text as the prime though not the sole repository of meaning and attends closely to the text. Intractable elements of the text are not ignored. We must recognize here that such an attitude to the text does not devalue the reader's own contribution to meaning. Such an attitude is demonstrated by David and somewhat less by Pierre. The latter does recognize that there are aspects of the text that he does not understand as part of any coherent meaning he can propose; but, unlike David, he is unable to find, develop, and test out the hypotheses that might resolve such incongruities.

5.2 The reader sets text aside.   Text is glossed over when it does not accord fully with the meaning being developed. Once initial hypotheses become established, text is used selectively to support such hypotheses. Readers like Petra and Angie seem to proceed in a linear fashion, directed by a frame general enough to allow them to accommodate or ignore intractable elements in the text.

In a study of how adult readers process expository text, Margaret MacLean (1986) distinguishes between those readers whose responses derive primarily from a close attendance to the text (who constantly turn to the text to check their understanding) and those readers whose responses derive primarily from their own knowledge (who rely more on their own knowledge to confirm their understanding of the text). In between are readers who integrate information derived from the text with their own knowledge of the topic. There are clear parallels between the readers described in 5.1 and 5.2 and MacLean's categories. It does not follow, however, that MacLean's "reader-bound" (as opposed to "text-bound") readers would read poetry in the same way as prose. Poems are much more self-contained and autonomous texts than are the expository texts used in such studies of comprehension, and they automatically invite a closer attendance to the text. At the same time, the charged language of poetry is more likely to evoke related experience.

Other Elements

6.1 Visualizing.   A few readers tend to visualize in order to understand what is occurring in the poem. Indications in the protocols are usually signaled by "I see" and "I have a picture." Generally, the protocols offer few clues to the internal state of the reader other than occasional expressions of puzzlement or some show of emotion about what they are reading.

6.2 Questions about vocabulary.   Some readers, almost as a matter of form, present a long list of words they feel uncertain about; others are more selective, tending to depend on contextual clues to work out the meanings of unfamiliar words or usage.

6.3 Attending to the title.   Titles appear to function as clues to meaning in a peripheral or subliminal way, only one of many clues that contribute to making sense of the poem. Titles are not attended to in any consistent way and only after the meaning of the poem has begun to emerge or when readers are searching for additional clues to guide their reading. I recall a reader who, reading "Cyclops," asked what a cyclops was only toward the end of the RAP. When she was provided with an explanation, she probably found it did not support any meaning she had in mind; she seemed to set the new information aside.

Other Protocol Features

There are aspects of the protocols that cannot be presented as elements; they are far less salient than most of the preceding elements and must be deduced from a combination of several factors in the RAPs. We may consider in the RAPs, for instance, the progress of the readings to decide whether subsequent readings expand initial observations or narrow them, or whether the readings are largely analytic or synthetic or both. We may decide whether a reader is involved in a process of prospective or retrospective structuring or, as Kintsch (1980) puts it, predicting or postdicting. We may inquire whether there are any connections between the patterns of response that emerge and evidence of metacognitive awareness in some of the protocols.[4]

These and related topics, while they clearly bear on the elements that make up the patterns of response, are best explored in the discussion that concludes this report, though they will certainly be touched on in the descriptions of the patterns that follow.

Patterns of Reading

The four readings of "Blackberry-Picking" reproduced in Chapter Three were chosen because they represent four distinctive patterns of reading discernible in the twenty-six RAPs I obtained. While it was clear, soon after the RAPs were transcribed, that these readers differed in the ways they went about making sense of poetry, the differences in their patterns of reading were not as easily apparent at first. The differences are most clear in the expectations they brought to the reading, the mind-set with which they approached the poem (as far as these expectations or mind-sets can be inferred from the protocols). The RAPs provide pictures of readers, for instance, who make concerted efforts after meaning, and readers who are anxious to close off discussion; readers who build an account of the poem relying primarily on their initial readings and stay close to these accounts through several readings, and readers who

4. I use the term *metacognitive awareness* to refer to the reader's awareness of the processes by which he or she goes about making sense of poetry. In these RAPs, that awareness is signaled by a self-monitoring of one's reading, particularly apparent when a reader deliberately considers a particular strategy: "Let me see what happens in the fall?"; or acknowledges, as David does, a particular difficulty: "That I'm not sure about. That's puzzling. Burned? . . . Why would they burn?" or "Why do I get the feeling it's a girl?"

weigh several interpretations through the process; readers who attend closely
to the text and constantly return to it to confirm their accounts of the poem,
and readers who do not. Moreover, these readers display the same behaviors
in both their protocols, even though the poems they are responding to differ
considerably in theme and structure. As we read an individual's protocol and
then proceed to read a second protocol from the same individual, we become
aware that there is a characteristic pattern we can ascribe to both protocols, a
pattern that transcends any differences that might be attributed to the differences in the poems.

The patterns described here are meant to type patterns of reading rather
than readers. They emerge from a growing familiarity with the protocols and
have been perceived as patterns simply because the behaviors and attitudes
that constitute them appear consistently in the pair of individual protocols and
can be discerned at times in the reader's contributions to the small-group discussions. The elements listed earlier in this chapter helped me to delineate
these patterns more clearly and to understand the variety of ways in which the
creation of meaning is influenced by the mind-set of the reader and the strategies that are brought to bear in the process.

A description of four broad patterns of reading poetry follows. These patterns account for the differences in reading patterns among the fourteen subjects. The descriptions of the four patterns are composites derived from the
behaviors of those readers who most nearly fit those patterns. No reader in any
category reads exactly as would be supposed from the description, and there
are some readers who do not fit exclusively into one of the four patterns. The
concluding section of this chapter makes clear the relations among these patterns of response. The four patterns of reading and, it follows, the four kinds
of readers are paraphrasers, thematizers, allegorizers, and problem solvers.

While I wish to characterize patterns of reading rather than readers, I have
found it more convenient to speak of kinds of readers. These patterns are
observable in individual readers' RAPs and are more easily described as the
acts of individual readers. The titles given to the patterns are basically labels
to hang descriptions on, and it is of course the descriptions rather than the
titles that define the patterns. I describe these patterns of reading poetry using
the main divisions of the list of elements set out earlier in this chapter (what
the reader brings to the poem, how the reader moves through the poem, closure, and the reader's relationship to the text) and discuss as well other protocol features.

Paraphrasers

What the Reader Brings to the Poem

I use the term *paraphrase* in the simple sense of restating the text in one's own
words. All readers paraphrase to some extent, but paraphrasers adopt a stance
where they see rendering the text in their own words as their sole responsibil-

ity. Somehow, they believe, paraphrasing will divulge meaning. A quite likely explanation for their reliance on this strategy lies in the fact that paraphrasing is a basic process in most classroom discussions of poetry, where it inevitably leads to other things. Again, during the preparatory small-group sessions and as a means of keeping the talk going, I encouraged the groups to go through the poem line by line (though not literally) in order to make out the plain sense or, to put it another way, to establish the text of the poem. That paraphrasers see no need to push, other than in a cursory way, beyond the literal meaning of the poem suggests a carryover from such classroom practice and points to a rather limited conception of what the reading of poetry is all about.

In some ways, then, paraphrasing is a wait-and-see strategy that says, "I have done what I am expected to do; is there anything else I must consider?" Usually, in the classroom setting, the teacher has suggested what the next step might be.

The Reader's Moves

I would describe the paraphraser's approach as frame-directed bottom-up processing. The paraphraser has usually worked out some sense of the topic of the poem from the initial reading. The topic is sufficiently general to allow the incorporation of most details from the text. At the same time, when paraphrasers encounter elements in the text that cannot be accommodated within their initial conception of what the poem is about, they might express some doubts about their ability to make sense of the poem; they are not, however, prepared to change their hypothesis to account for this new input. Quite likely, such intractable elements do not make sense while viewed from within the context in which these readers are working. At the same time, their previous experience with poetic text may not encourage them to consider alternative contexts within which intractable elements might be accommodated. And in any case, where is the alternative context to come from? They may as well stay with what appears to be working for most aspects of the poem. The effect of the initial context they have assumed persists with paraphrasers much more than it does with other readers.

The paraphraser appears to be involved in a process of fleshing out an initial impression, an initial frame rather than a hypothesis. The process is unlike hypothesis making in the sense that the hypothesis here is not truly tentative; it is subject to very little modification. Paraphrasers seem to feel the need to make up their minds about what's going on simply because they take a detailed run through the poem, retelling the facts of the poem, breaking it up into smaller portions.

After the first detailed retelling, usually after the second reading of the text, each subsequent reading is merely a consolidation and a briefer account of what was said earlier. Occasionally, puzzling aspects will be encountered but are set aside as not making sense or merely glossed over in the process of turning to something else. Paraphrasers are usually satisfied with their accounts of the poem, even if they are aware of aspects of the poem they have not been able to explain. They are not, however, prepared to reconsider their accounts in order to deal with these aspects of the poem.

There are readers who are not "pure" paraphrasers in the sense that they do not see a paraphrase of the poem as the sole object of their reading. Paraphrase is used in these cases as a way of establishing the context and considering the possibilities of meaning. These belong to another category of readers. There are other readers who paraphrase to a considerable extent; however, because they adopt an interpretive frame only tentatively, they are prepared to shift their ground and reconsider the context with which they are working when they encounter parts of the text that just do not fit in.

Closure

Paraphrasers seem anxious to close soon after their first or second retelling of the poem. They appear to believe that they have done what they set out to do and that no further purpose would be served by going through the poem again. "That's about it," Angie says quite often in the latter half of her protocol. Paraphrasers are aware of gaps in their retelling of the poem but do not believe that another reading will be of any help.

Some paraphrasers seem to feel the need to close with a moral or a lesson, a thematic statement of some kind, but such a statement is just tagged on; the poem is not reexamined in terms of this new idea—it is a concluding idea.

The Reader's Relationship to Poetic Text

As must be apparent already, paraphrasers deal with text serially, retelling as they go along, and either filling out the initial frame they have set for the poem or, if the poem has a narrative structure, relating events in a temporal or causal sequence. Non-narrative text requires a great deal more inferencing on the part of the reader, guided by an initial impression or frame, and often that initial impression or frame inadequately accounts for what is sequentially revealed by the text. Paraphrasers, however, do not feel bound to account for all aspects of the text; inevitably, there are gaps in their reading.

Other Protocol Features

The approach to text is serial and analytic, working from an initial impression or frame. If there is synthesis, it involves merely tacking on a theme rather than drawing it out. In terms of the goals they set for themselves, paraphrasers are successful readers; but their goals are limited. For this reason primarily, they are reluctant readers of poetry. Of the four readers whose RAPs are reproduced in this book, Angie is the one who relies most on this way of reading. Overall, of the fourteen readers, two were clearly paraphrasers.

Thematizers

The terms *theme finders* or *theme seekers* would more accurately describe this category of readers but are unfortunately unwieldy. I have in mind readers who read a poem intent on finding a theme. Of the four readers whose RAPs are included in this study, Pierre most closely represents this way of reading. Overall, two of the fourteen readers revealed a thematizing pattern in their RAPs. Other readers, though, tend to operate partly in this mode.

What the Reader Brings to the Text

Thematizers see their task as one of finding a theme for the poem. The theme is conceived as a statement, usually a generalization, about life, nature, animals, landscapes, or the human condition. What especially characterizes thematizers is a notion that underlying the complexity of a poem is a rather simple theme and that it is the reader's task to discover it and bring it to light. For this reason especially, thematizers appear to take stabs at meaning in the expectation that somehow the theme will thus be tapped.

The Reader's Moves

A thematizer's protocol is usually disjointed; there appears to be no sense of a developing inquiry into the meaning of the poem or the working out of a hypothesis or initial impression. Thus the thematizer's protocol does not appear to be directed by a controlling frame. Neither is there an attempt to paraphrase as a means of establishing the plain sense of the text. In fact, thematizers' protocols read like a series of probes for meaning, each one seemingly unrelated to the others and punctuated by long pauses.

When invited to report what he or she is thinking during these pauses, the thematizer is most likely to respond that nothing is happening during these pauses, that is, nothing that he or she is able to report. What appears to be happening is that the reader, unsure of the next step, is glancing through the text in the hope of finding something meaningful to say—in this case, a theme-like statement. Attention is focused primarily at the local sentence level in the hope that one of those sentences might suggest an image or meaning that will "break the code."

Thematizers work actively with text, anxious to come to meaning but at the same time unable to find a theme that makes for a satisfactory reading of the poem. Working mostly at the local level, they do not appear to have an overall sense of the poem against which they can test out a hypothesis. There is no cumulative buildup of meaning as one locally developed hypothesis is set aside in order to develop another one for another segment of the poem.

Closure

A closing note is sounded in the form of "nothing else comes to me" or "that's all I get now." There is a strong impression that the reader and the text have not connected, that a coherent account has not emerged. The poem has revealed several possible meanings but none that are satisfactory to the reader in accounting for the various local meanings that have come up.

The Reader's Relationship to Poetic Text

Thematizers work actively with text searching for meaning; however, while the text is attended to for meaning, it is set aside as soon as a satisfactory theme is discovered.

Other Protocol Features

The approach is generally analytic. Meaning is to be discovered as one searches through the text. In terms of the objectives they set for themselves, thematizers are unsuccessful readers.

Allegorizers

I use the term *allegorize* to describe the behavior of those readers who approach a poem as though it embodies symbolically real-life events or beliefs. In other words, allegorizers see their task as having to work out the equivalence between the poem and the real world. Five of the fourteen readers belonged in this category; Petra's RAPs most clearly illustrate the pattern.

What the Reader Brings to the Text

In essence, allegorizers approach a poem as though it represents an extended statement about life. Unlike thematizers, they look at the poem as a whole and approach the poem with an overall impression or frame that guides their reading. They are similar to paraphrasers in that respect, except that they conceive their task as more than merely reporting the plain sense of the poem. Instead, they work on formulating a statement about life as it is presented by and can be construed from the poem.

Often such statements represent stock notions carried over from past experience, particularly past experiences with literature. Allegorizers approach the poem with a strong expectation that the poem will make sense. They seem to direct the process by a controlling idea to a much greater extent than other readers do; that is, they assume responsibility for making sense of the poem.

The Reader's Moves

Most allegorizers work from a strong feeling or intuition about the poem. "I get this feeling of loneliness," says one. Their basic move is to formulate a generalization about life or nature and develop that generalization to accord with details of the poem. The process is one of aligning aspects of the text with aspects of the meaning being developed: this in the text means that in life. Textual details that do not accord with the interpretation being developed are generally set aside or realigned to fit the interpretation. Such realigning is not necessarily a severe distortion of the poem's basic meaning, because allegorizers' initial impressions and generalizations reflect a broad understanding of the poem, broad enough to gloss over aspects of the text that appear inconsistent with the meaning being developed. In their initial runs through the poem, allegorizers tend not to be overly specific in their interpretations, preferring to stay at a level of generalization that will allow the text to fit the meaning.

Those initial impressions prove to be a powerful factor in determining the reading of the poem. They appear to develop from an open stance to the poem's meaning and are hard to shake once they appear to accord with the poem's basic details. "I keep getting that," says one reader referring to a persisting early impression, and later, "That's what I get." No two ways about it.

It seems that allegorizers are most themselves when they are dealing with non-narrative text in poetry, where a pattern of relationships dominates and can be understood by its application to similar patterns in the world. A narrative framework invites paraphrase, and it takes an effort of mind not to dwell primarily on the narrative and to go on to seek analogous patterns of experience.

Closure

Allegorizers tend to be satisfied with their efforts in making sense of the poem. They are aware of gaps in their interpretations but do not seem to believe that these indicate flaws in their basic interpretations.

The Reader's Relationship to Poetic Text

Allegorizers appear to read the text with an eye to its general contours. They tend to twist the text to fit the meaning they are creating, but some allegorizers are less oblivious than others to the demands they are making on the text, acknowledging they are not sure of this and that aspect of their interpretation. At the same time, they are not willing to develop and consider a hypothesis that might better accommodate the inconsistencies they sense.

Other Protocol Features

Allegorizers' approach to text is basically synthetic. They draw on those aspects of text that support the meaning they are constructing and ignore those that do not; at the same time, they are able to pick up central issues and are generally confident they have understood the poem. They are analytic in their approach to the extent that they are able to sort out and fit the text to their meaning.

Problem Solvers

Problem solvers are a group of readers, four out of the fourteen, whose approach to making sense of poetry is to try a variety of strategies. While all our readers were involved to some degree in a problem-solving task, this group of readers adopted a stance and employed strategies typical of successful problem solvers.

What the Reader Brings to the Text

Problem solvers, more than the readers in the other categories, approach the poem with enthusiasm for the task ahead. They are alert to possibilities of meaning and to connections between the poem and their own experience. Personal associations set off by the poem lead back into the poem rather than out of the poem into dwelling on the personal experience.

The Reader's Moves

Problem solvers do not all operate in the same way. If they share a common trait, it is a refusal to settle immediately on meaning and, rather, to be tentative in their formulations of meaning. It is not that they do not trust themselves as readers; it is rather that they see poetry as a complex artifact that does not easily reveal its meaning. Thus they are tolerant of ambiguity, willing to postpone dealing with apparent blocks to understanding until they are ready to deal with them. The readiness is most likely to be demonstrated in taking another run through the poem in the hope of achieving a perspective that might disentangle the difficulties and eliminate the ambiguity. But they are not easily satisfied; time and time again, they announce their puzzlement and return to problematical areas. Problem solvers also share a common approach in that they use a variety of strategies to make sense of poetry. The chief strategy is setting and testing several hypotheses in the effort toward meaning.

Problem solvers, almost immediately after the first reading, announce a hypothesis about the general meaning of the poem. This hypothesis is more often than not rejected when it does not fit the information being derived from the poem. A second hypothesis is then tentatively developed and tested. This is a considered, unhasty move. Difficulties in comprehending portions of text are not set aside immediately but are attended to. If the current hypothesis cannot accommodate these difficulties, the hypothesis is modified, set aside provisionally, or abandoned; or else those difficulties that cannot be resolved are set aside to be returned to later. The hypotheses are not merely pulled out of thin air. Problem solvers probe their own experience for analogous clues and search actively through the text for clues as to what is happening.

There are other strategies as well. Problem solvers are distinguished from other readers in the variety of means they employ in working toward understanding a poem. Thus they turn as much as other readers to feelings and intuitions to direct their reading. Like other readers, they paraphrase, not as the major strategy but as one more means of enhancing their understanding.

More than the other readers, problems solvers tend to visualize what is happening in the poem: they get "flashes," images, and pictures.

Closure

Problem solvers generally tend to delay closure. Whatever tentative interpretations they may have worked out they tend to see as inadequate unless they can account for those aspects of the poem they have found difficult to understand or accommodate. Like readers in other categories, they sense there is something in the poem they "just haven't got" or "can't get," but unlike those other readers, problem solvers consider it their responsibility to find out. Such delay of closure also probably derives from their having experienced poetry as a continuing unfolding of meaning. For them, a poem is never fully understood. As one struggling problem solver announced during a small-group discussion of a poem, "I always only get the meaning at night." She is referring to the later rereading of the poem required by her journal-writing task.

The Reader's Relationship with Poetic Text

More than among the other kinds of readers, there is an active interplay between text and reader. Problem solvers do not abandon the text once they feel they have a workable hypothesis; neither do they dwell at the level of text without one or more tentative hypotheses in mind. Thus, because of this respect for the integrity of the text, problem solvers almost always catch their own misreadings or miscues.

Other Protocol Features

Problem solvers' approach to the text is primarily synthetic. The effort after meaning is directed by an overall awareness of several possibilities of meaning and a gradual narrowing down of those possibilities. The stance is tentative. Of all readers interviewed, problem solvers appeared to be most aware of their own processes in reading poetry.[5]

Summary: Patterns and Elements

A thorough familiarity with the RAPs has helped me work out and describe the patterns of reading discussed in the previous sections. My understanding of these readers' patterns has been helped by a familiarity with a considerable amount of supplementary data: other RAPs, written journal entries, transcripts of small-group discussions, stream-of-consciousness written protocols, and personal interviews. I am sure my sense of these patterns has grown also from personal contact with these readers over two years. Such supplementary data have in general confirmed that these students' individual patterns of reading are not at odds with the ways in which they write about a poem or talk about it in small groups. A confirming note has also been sounded by several hundred teachers of English who, on various occasions, have heard my account of the patterns of reading and observed that their pupils do read in the ways I have described.

5. Readers may have noticed that I use the term *patterns of reading* rather than *patterns of response*, even though *patterns of response* is more inclusive. I should point out by way of explanation that the patterns that distinguish these readers one from the other have emerged primarily in terms of how they read rather than how they respond. But I must insist that how one reads is a large part of, and to be realistic, inseparable from how one responds. To make more of the distinction at this stage would not be helpful.

Table 1

ELEMENTS IN THE PROCESS		PATTERNS OF READING			
		P	**T**	**A**	**PS**
What the Reader Brings to the Poem *A Reader's Expectations of How a Poem Means*					
1.1	A poem is a complex way of saying something simple.	⋆	⋆	o	—
1.2	All aspects of a poem contribute to the meaning of a poem.	—	—	o	⋆
A Reader's Expectations of What a Poem Means					
2.1	A poem usually represents one of several stock themes.	✓	⋆	✓	—
2.2	A poem embodies a complex meaning that is never fully realized.	—	—	—	⋆
Prior World Knowledge					
3.1	The reader is open to personal experience.	—	✓	✓	⋆
3.2	The reader does not draw on personal experience.	✓	—	—	—
How the Reader Moves Through the Poem					
4.1	Bottom-up processing of text	✓	⋆	—	—
4.2	Frame-directed bottom-up processing of text	⋆	—	—	✓
4.3	Top-down processing directed by a strong initial impression	—	—	⋆	—
4.4	Top-down processing of text—tentative frame	—	—	—	⋆
4.5	Hypothesis formation—single	✓	—	⋆	—
4.6	Hypothesis formation—multiple	—	⋆	—	⋆
4.7	Drawing on personal experience	—	✓	✓	⋆
4.8	Early closure	⋆	⋆	—	—
4.9	Delayed closure	—	—	✓	⋆

P = paraphrasers
T = thematizers
A = allegorizers
PS = problem solvers

⋆ Element is a distinguishing characterisic of pattern.
✓ Element features in the pattern.
o Element may or may not feature in the pattern.
+ Yet to be determined.
— Not found.

In developing my accounts of the patterns of reading, I have benefited considerably from the observations and insights of several graduate students and research assistants who helped me in this study. As they became familiar with the RAPs, they independently confirmed my reading of the RAPs and the patterns they represent. Their confirmation extended as well to the identification of the elements in the RAPs and attribution of them to specific portions or aspects of the RAPs. These recorders used a form to note elements that they could identify in each RAP (see left side of Table 1). The elements

Table 1 continued

ELEMENTS IN THE PROCESS	PATTERNS OF READING			
	P	**T**	**A**	**PS**
The Reader's Relationship to Poetic Text				
5.1 The reader attends closely to the text.	—	✓	—	⋆
5.2 The reader sets text aside.	✓	—	✓	—
Other Elements				
6.1 Visualizing	o	✓	o	✓
6.2 Questions about vocabulary	✓	✓	—	—
6.3 Attending to the title	+	+	+	✓
Other Protocol Features				
7.1 Analytical approach	⋆	⋆	—	—
7.2 Synthetic approach	—	—	⋆	—
7.3 Synthetic-analytic approach	—	—	—	⋆
7.4 Prospective structuring	+	+	+	+
7.5 Retrospective structuring	+	+	+	+
7.6 Metacognitive awareness	✓	—	✓	⋆

P = paraphrasers ⋆ Element is a distinguishing characterisic of pattern.
T = thematizers ✓ Element features in the pattern.
A = allegorizers o Element may or may not feature in the pattern.
PS = problem solvers + Yet to be determined.
— Not found.

listed in this form, drawn from my analysis of the RAPs, correspond to those discussed in previous sections of this chapter.

I believe it is not difficult to achieve a high degree of consensus on the particular pattern of reading represented in a RAP when such identifications are the result of holistic readings deriving from considerable familiarity with the RAP. I have also argued that these elements do not appear as discrete items in a RAP but must be derived from such holistic readings and from a degree of familiarity with the protocol. Thus, in presenting this form, it is not my intention to offer a quick, totally reliable way of reading patterns in the RAPs. What the form does offer is an easier way of checking readings of the RAPs and establishing similarities and differences among the various RAPs. The form can also be used to profile the elements as they are identified in each RAP and to note how they correspond to the four patterns of reading. Some of the elements are characteristic of one particular pattern; others figure in more than one. Elements other than those I have listed can be identified in the protocols.

On the right side of Table 1, I have superposed on the form a chart that represents my attempt to outline the relations between the elements in the process of reading poetry and the patterns of reading. It is important to recall that, with respect to each element, reader's stances and acts fall along a range between two extremes. Thus the charting of the patterns cum elements in Table 1 inevitably distorts somewhat but is useful, I believe, for highlighting the differences among the four types of readers as they attempt to make sense of poetry.

I have described how I proceeded to confirm my readings of the RAPs and the descriptions of the four patterns of reading. A logical next step might be to test these findings on a wider scale and with a careful concern for establishing a high degree of reliability among independent reviewers of RAPs. This report should make such a study more likely. I have hesitated to move in that direction for this study simply because such reliability depends on establishing a set of markers and a precise set of definitions for such markers. Such a move would be in the direction of—to adapt a well-known observation by James Moffett (1968, 23)—reducing reality to manageable proportions, that is, trading a loss of reality for a gain in control. Readers will appreciate, I am sure, that the RAPs are not that easily reducible.

As the RAPs are sorted into one or another of the four reading patterns with increasing consistency, and as the elements become more reliable means of establishing such sorting, one can propose such distinctions among ways of reading with a high degree of conviction. But there is a consistency and convincingness also in the interrelations among the patterns themselves. The patterns of reading I have described make sense in that they cohere, in that there appear to be no inherent contradictions among them, and because, as I show in the final chapter, they have an explanatory power.

When we examine the patterns to determine how they relate to each other, we notice that the readers in this study proceed in one of two ways. As they try to make sense of the poem, some proceed generally bottom-up, attending primarily to local cues at the sentence level, and composing meaning serially as paraphrasers do, or searching for clues to meaning as thematizers do. Both problem solvers and allegorizers differ from the other readers in that they work primarily top-down, attending to the text with one or more possibilities of meaning in mind, and confirming hunches or crystallizing meaning as evidence from the text accumulates. In making this distinction, I am not oblivious to the fact that the initial reading of a poem is primarily bottom-up, even though some readers are more likely than others to have assembled cues that point to likely organizing frames. I should hasten to add, however, that none of the readers interrupt this first reading (by the interviewer) to say what they are thinking, nor were they expected to. Figure 1 illustrates these approaches to poetic text.

One can, of course, discern certain similarities and differences among reading patterns. Unlike paraphrasers, thematizers may not feel the need to

Figure 1

Problem Solvers	Attend *primarily* to global cues—top-down
Allegorizers	
Thematizers	Attend *primarily* to local cues—bottom-up
Paraphrasers	

verbalize their understanding of the plain sense of the text and in fact are concerned primarily to probe the text for meaning, to interpret. Allegorizers work from a notion of the plain sense of the text but are guided by an initial feeling or sense of what the poem is about. Like thematizers, they attend to local clues but do so in the context of the overall sense of what the poem is about. Problem solvers indicate in their protocols that they have a general grasp of the plain sense of the text but are just as much aware of aspects that do not at first glance appear to make sense. Like thematizers, they are alert to possibilities of meaning at the local level but, again, within the context of several likely emerging meanings. Like allegorizers, problem solvers attend to what they feel or sense is happening but, unlike them, are not primarily guided by such impressions and remain concerned to accommodate seemingly intractable elements in the poem.

There are other similarities and dissimilarities as well. Both thematizers and problem solvers do not settle on meaning quickly; thematizers cast around in the poem in the hope that a satisfactory meaning will emerge, and problem solvers work through the poem open to several possibilities of meaning. On the other hand, paraphrasers and allegorizers proceed serially, allegorizers fitting the text to the meaning they have found or are hoping to find beyond the text, and paraphrasers retelling the details of the poem in conformance with a satisfactory generalization.

If we consider the patterns in terms of the elements that constitute them, the differences in the patterns are primarily differences of degree rather than kind; some readers conceive the task of making sense of poetry in far more challenging terms than others. Thus the paraphraser perceives that task as going not much further than making out the plain sense, whereas the problem solver is unwilling to settle easily on a meaning. Both the thematizer and the allegorizer are somewhat more ambitious than the paraphraser in the goals they set for themselves as readers: the thematizer searches actively for a stock theme that is "concealed" in the poem, and the allegorizer, working from a strong initial impression of the poem, fleshes it out by fitting in as many aspects of the poem as can be accommodated.

Overall, these differences in patterns of reading could be explained as the result of different positions on a gamut of expectations of what constitutes meaning in poetry and what one's responsibilities are as a reader. In describing these patterns to teachers and pointing out their interrelations, I have sometimes found it useful to describe the search for meaning in poetry in terms of prospecting for gold. Both paraphrasers and allegorizers map the territory—paraphrasers with little sense of what lies beneath the surface and allegorizers reading the topography for a fairly general picture of the underground ore formations. Thematizers are miners who act on hunches to dig in various places in the hope of finding a rich vein. Problem solvers are both surveyors and miners; they scan and they probe, are not anxious to close, and know there is more.

5

Implications for Classroom Practice

The intention of this study has been to track the processes by which adolescent readers go about making sense of poetry. A methodology for studying response to a poem as that response occurs has been proposed and tested, four patterns of reading have been described, and a list of elements that help chart these patterns has been delineated.

There are obvious limitations to this study. In the first place, I cannot insist that the patterns observed in the RAPs of fourteen readers and the elements that compose these patterns are generalizable to all or even most adolescent readers of poetry. Second, I am aware that I am describing what occurs only in the initial stages of the encounter between adolescent reader and poem. Third, the information recorded in the RAPs is limited by what the reader is able and willing to report on and, despite all the preparation involved, is influenced to some extent by the presence of the interviewer, who may have inadvertently encouraged or discouraged certain lines of inquiry. Fourth, there are aspects of response to poetry that are not easily inferred from the protocols: the "experiential" aspects of response and the aesthetic judgments that are not easily pointed to in the protocols but cannot be deemed absent simply because the pupils did not report them. (David's RAP, when compared with the others', demonstrates that some readers are more willing than others to report on their experience of the poem.) Despite these limitations, the explanatory power of the four patterns has been acknowledged by most teachers with whom I have discussed them and who are concerned to understand the reading behaviors of their pupils. Some of these teachers have even confessed that they recognized their own reading styles in these accounts.

This study raises several issues, two of which have direct relevance to classroom practice and will be considered at some length. The first is, Are there explanations in classroom practice that may account for the differences in patterns of reading? What classroom situations, for instance, make these patterns functional? The second is, How does one take account of these various ways of reading when one teaches poetry?

Differences in Reading Patterns: Likely Sources

In raising this question I do not wish to argue that individual patterns are determined primarily by what happens in poetry classrooms. My argument is rather that classroom practice inevitably dictates how a poem must be read and makes some goals for reading poetry more useful and productive (in terms of what seems to be valued) than others. Travers (1984, 378) in her review of research on poetry in the classroom, cites a number of studies to suggest that

> The majority of pupils in a class will, regardless of their differing personalities, respond according to the preference indicated by the teacher's questioning behavior and the teacher's way of receiving pupils' responses. In other words, pupils tend to learn what teachers teach, though some teachers may be unaware of what they are teaching.

The major source of differences in reading patterns lies in the expectations brought by the students to the reading of poetry. Pupils' notions of what constitutes meaning in poetry, where meaning is to be found, and what is involved in reading for meaning will influence considerably their approaches to the reading of a poem. Thus, the readers in this study ranged between those who read as though the poem was a complex way of stating a simple theme and those who read as though the complexity itself was an indication of a deeper significance that is not easily and immediately realized. Expectations such as these and the different ways in which these pupils see their responsibilities as readers most likely have their roots in classroom practices.

Thus a classroom climate that places a premium on eliciting information, getting the "facts" of the poem right, may encourage a bottom-up, text-based approach to the reading of a poem. Such an approach takes little account of readers' contributions to the making of meaning, that is, of the notion of reading as a transaction between reader and text. In such a classroom, students may tend to discount the experience the poem evokes for them and not feel encouraged to make connections between what they read and what they have experienced and know. We may speculate, for instance, that paraphrasers see their responsibility mainly as reproducing the plain sense of the text because teacher questioning has worked primarily at eliciting a paraphrase; interpretation has usually been the teacher's prerogative or at best has been directed by the teacher's line of questioning. I have argued elsewhere (Dias 1979) that much classroom teaching of poetry seems directed toward building a dependence on the teacher as interpreter. To use Graves' (1981) analogy concerning writing, the teacher owns the poem, the pupils merely rent it.

It is for the same reason, I suspect, that thematizers take stabs at meaning. Particular lines of classroom questioning that follow a teacher's agenda for explicating a poem can encourage guesswork. Unfortunately, the competitive climate of many classrooms does not encourage the kind of guessing—hypothesis testing—that is exploratory, tentative, and collaborative. Douglas Barnes, in his study of teacher-pupil classroom talk, shows how many teachers, on receiving an acceptable explanation from one pupil, will proceed as though all the other pupils were at the same stage in their understanding of the lesson (Barnes, Britton, and Rosen 1971). It is likely that in poetry lessons pupils get used to hearing a teacher accept answers or offer explanations whose genesis they cannot quite fathom but that make eminent sense ("It's so simple when *you* explain it!"). They most likely feel that poetry will never make sense to them and come to believe that the only useful strategy is to make good guesses that may eventually find their target.

It is a simple trial-and-error approach, an approach developed in a teacher-dominated classroom where the challenge is to find the teacher's meanings rather than work out one's own. Such developments are not surprising in classrooms where students, when asked a question, are given little time to reflect and explore tentatively simply because the teacher (as the students know) proceeds along a predetermined line of questions that call for particular answers. Undirected by a teacher's questions, as in a RAP interview, a thematizer can only take stabs at meaning, probes that do not appear to take account of preceding finds. It could not be otherwise in those many classrooms that require the right answer too quickly.

I seem to be arguing that patterns of reading are largely determined by a particular classroom climate and style of teaching. This is only partly true. It is readers who, for whatever reason, decide what are their responsibilities as readers; and these responsibilities can contract to making out the plain sense or widen to include a working out of the analogies between the poem and real life, as is the case with allegorizers. Classroom procedures can either constrain or extend readers' notions of their responsibilities as readers. Information I have collected on classroom procedures that prevail in the teaching of poetry (my own observations, a survey of high school English teachers, and a review of methodology textbooks)[1] suggests that the teaching of poetry is largely teacher-dominated, that pupils on the whole have little or no opportunity or incentive to make sense of a poem for themselves. Thus, while one can point to certain practices in such classrooms that may encour-

1. Since I wrote this, that is, over the last seven years, I have noticed that curriculum documents and articles in journals such as *Language Arts, English Journal, Reading Teacher, Journal of Reading,* and in Canada, *English Quarterly* reveal an increasing awareness of reader-response theory and its relevance for classroom practice. However, with few exceptions, there remains a reluctance by and large to assign readers *full* ownership of and responsibility for their readings. While most teachers recognize the need to invite and acknowledge student responses, many of them are at the same time concerned to guide them toward preferred readings.

age paraphrasing or thematizing, one must also recognize that such class-rooms hardly provide fertile soil for the development of a problem-solving approach to reading a poem. In fact, problem solvers are at a decided disad-vantage in such classrooms. When I returned to the school a year later to obtain a new set of RAPs from the same pupils, it was David, whom I have categorized as a problem solver, who complained that he did not feel encour-aged to contribute to classroom discussion of poetry. His initial observations, he was often told by the teacher, had little to do with the poem and were there-fore disruptive. It is not difficult to see how David's tentative offerings might not have fitted in with the set agenda of the teacher's line of questioning.

If a problem-solving approach to reading poetry persists despite the kind of teaching that would discourage it, is problem solving then a pattern of read-ing that operates successfully (and is thus confirmed) in other reading activi-ties (literary and nonliterary, classroom and nonclassroom)? Is a problem-solving approach to poetry a particular manifestation of what would more inclusively be called a particular learning style? To shift the question slightly, Are these patterns of reading particular only to the reading of poetry or literary text? These are interesting questions. The beginnings of an answer lie in designing studies that would assemble more comprehensive data on readers' reading and learning styles, including readers' approaches to nonlit-erary texts.

The data I now have do not reveal any demonstrable link between these readers' approaches to making sense of poetry and any aspect of their personal backgrounds that one might consider particularly relevant. I notice, for instance, that in their work in other areas of the school curriculum, none of the four kinds of readers distinguish themselves in any particular way that would suggest that their patterns of reading quite likely carry over to and make a cen-tral and discernible difference to academic performance in these other areas. One would think they would. If they do not, is it likely that the majority of secondary school pupils unconsciously subvert *their* ways of making sense of what they read and attempt to acquire and practice the ways of making sense that are taught explicitly and implicitly in lessons? In most teacher-led class-es, pupils are most likely to adopt ways of reading that are invited by and prove functional in their particular classroom contexts. Thus, in the regular large-group exchange of the classroom, David will not verbalize his prob-lem-solving strategies because they disrupt the mode of inquiring that the teacher has prescribed; and he will soon work out what is expected of him. Even in the small-group work, David more often than not gives way to the will of the group and does not force his point of view on them. His contribu-tions, however, are always helpful. It is the RAPs that allow him full scope for the problem-solving strategies he employs. Here is Rick, a fourteen-year-old in England, who reads in a problem-solving pattern, reflecting (during a post-RAP interview) on how he functions within the small group in their poetry discussion:

[In] the small groups, yes, I [take] their ideas as well.

I sit back and I don't say anything until they have pooled all their ideas at the same level as mine and start building a pattern up and have my thoughts on the side and merge the two so that I start building up.

Not until I've got a fairly good picture and then I say, "Hey, look what's happening," and then we start talking and another batch of ideas start to form.

In other words, Rick does not involve the members of the group in his own exploratory assembling of ideas (including the ones his group is contributing) until he has arrived at a feasible hypothesis, "a fairly good picture," at which time he presents his account to the group "and another batch of ideas start to form." That latter phrase nicely points up his notion that such joining together of ideas is only a stage in the process of arriving at a fuller reading. I have cited Rick here and later in this chapter because he appears to be so fully aware of his own processes as a reader of poetry.

Patterns of reading, then, are very much directed by the contexts within which these students are asked to make sense of poetry. In large-group teacher-directed situations, individual patterns of reading must give way to the ways of reading that are implicit in the teachers' questions and procedures. In the small-group context, individual ways of making sense must give some way to the direction and goals of the collaborative effort—a matter of jointly negotiating meaning. Some readers are more expansive in such small-group situations than they are in the individual RAP context; most others appear to have a lot more to say during the RAPs than one would expect from what they contribute in the small group. The individual patterns of reading discerned in the RAPs emerge, I would argue, primarily because the RAP context invites students to proceed confidently in *their* ways of making sense of a poem. Thus it is quite likely that in many classrooms some of these individual, private ways of making sense are not likely to have much play or scope and are therefore less likely to be exercised.

The goals and expectations that making sense implies are, I believe, largely defined by what happens in English lessons. At the same time, there is little evidence to suggest that individual patterns of reading derive solely or even mainly from certain classroom practices. The fact that pupils showed different patterns of reading even though they were taught by the same teacher, and had been taught in the past by teachers who did not differ noticeably in their philosophy and approach to the teaching of poetry, suggests that far more detailed case histories of readers need to be constructed before clear links can be established between these patterns and teaching styles.

The larger scope of inquiry may reveal that these are patterns not merely of reading words but of reading the world: understanding one's experiences, interpreting events, perceiving reality. I am not really stretching a point and am reminded of Susanne Langer's notion of literature as "virtual experience" (1953, 215) and of D. W. Harding's book on poetry, *Experience into Words*

(1963). When Rosenblatt (1978) speaks of the "lived-through experience of the work" and Harding (1937) distinguishes between reader as participant and reader as spectator, they have in mind much more than the act of attending only to words on the page. Could one say that these patterns of reading indicate habits of mind? that one tends to "read" events or experiences in one or some combination of any of four ways: linear sequentially (paraphrasing), in a trial-and-error fashion hoping to find an appropriate fit (thematizing), holistic-intuitively (allegorizing), or holistic-systematically (problem solving)? In a follow-up to this study, when some of these pupils were asked individually to talk about two paintings (by Edward Hopper and Paul Klee), their commentaries suggested patterns of viewing and interpreting similar to their ways of reading a poem. This is not entirely surprising when one considers that making sense of a poem may have just as much affinity with making sense of a painting (with ways of looking and seeing) as it does with shaping and assembling the images and meanings one draws from the text. And yet much of the research on comprehending literary text has proceeded as though one is speaking only and merely of the comprehension of what are ultimately words on a page.

Implications for Teaching Poetry: Some Suggestions

While the likely influences for the patterns of reading I have described are not easily identifiable, the fact of differing patterns of reading sets a challenge for classroom practice. Too often and for too long the teaching of poetry has proceeded as though all the pupils in the classroom respond to a poem in the same way; that is, that they have read the same poem. Some practices favor one kind of approach to reading poetry more than others; certain kinds of readers are ill served by some approaches. As I have mentioned, problem solvers are treated as erratic and irresponsible readers when a teacher seeks to direct a particular reading of a poem. Paraphrasers and allegorizers find it least difficult to cope with traditional, teacher-directed approaches to the study of poetry. Thematizers, on the other hand, find it difficult to "get on track" and join the general discussion.

It would seem reasonable, then, that any approach to the teaching of poetry should take account of differences in reading patterns and should help students to develop confidence in their own resources as readers of poetry and, it follows, to continually test and develop their own strategies as readers of poetry. The following suggestions are made with these concerns primarily in mind and take account as well of classroom constraints and the demands of official school programs.

Small-Group Work

The approach least likely to meet the foregoing concerns is what I would call the full-frontal approach, with the teacher at the head of the class directing the reading and interpretation of the poem for the class. An approach that takes account of differences in reading patterns and the need to help develop autonomous readers of poetry is the small-group approach described in Chapter Two, which preceded the collection of the RAPs. Of course, taking account of individual patterns of reading is not that crucial an issue if one argues that the teacher's role is to model and enforce an ideal pattern of reading, whatever that may be. There are, however, other just as important reasons for suggesting the small-group discussion approach:

1. Undirected small-group discussion clearly assigns responsibility for making sense of the poem to the reader. "An approach is personal or it is nothing," says Leavis (1948, 68).

2. Readers are made aware of the several possibilities of meaning and are more likely to learn to live with ambiguity and to postpone closure.

3. Readers learn to tolerate and consider other ways of reading and, in the process, reevaluate over a period of time their own ways of reading.

4. As their observations and evaluations are considered by the group, readers may develop some degree of confidence in their own responses.

5. It is more likely that readers will evoke a personal experience of the poem within the relative security of the small group than within the large-group format. Readers are also more likely to announce the feelings and associations called up by the poem, which are a vital part of "the lived-through experience of the work" (to cite Rosenblatt [1978] once more).

There are other reasons, most of which have already been argued in my discussion of the place of small-group work in helping adolescent readers become independent readers of poetry. Not least of all is the positive attitudes toward the reading and study of poetry that such an approach promotes (see Bryant 1984; Dias 1992).

The Role of the Teacher

In several places in this report I have stressed the importance of the teacher's moving out of the way of the transaction between readers and poems. This is more easily said than done, particularly in contexts that stress evaluation and the teacher's powerful role in determining who gets what. If students are to assume responsibility for making sense of poetry, then teachers need to signal in every way that students do indeed have the right and the responsibility. Thus, at the end of the small-group reporting-back sessions I have described, I often had to refuse to assume the role of someone who had all the answers to questions that had puzzled the students. They had to realize that my questions were just as genuine as theirs, that I hoped they had answers to some of the questions the poem and their accounts had raised for me. Such a stance must under no circumstances take on a semblance of play-acting or appear even faintly patronizing. As Michael Hayhoe (1984, 43) puts it,

> Having to admit that poems cannot always be pinned down or "solved," even by us, may be disconcerting for us and for our students. It can also be a releasing discovery, a means of showing that teachers have as much right to be puzzled by a poem as any other human being and that poems have rights of ambiguity and inexhaustibility like any other artistic venture.

Students must come to realize that to be left with questions is a far better state to be in than not to have any questions at all. As I write this, I recall Nadia's comment during the small-group discussion of a poem. As the group was considering what they might report to the large group, Nadia (who is fourteen) hopes that the other groups will not agree with what they have to say:

> I hate it when they agree . . . Then at night; you don't . . . you don't expand on the poem. How do you know what to write about [in your journal]?

I take particular delight in Nadia's comment: she values disagreement primarily because it stimulates further inquiry, a looking-again, and is quite in opposition to a consensus-seeking pattern that tends to operate in much classroom teaching of poetry.

Unfortunately, getting out of the way is more easily said than done. My experience is that even when they are making every effort not to direct students' responses, teachers appear unable to contain a strong urge to nudge in the right direction, so to speak. Such tendencies are apparent even in the RAPs when the interviewer, particularly after a long pause, cannot resist responding directively. Such a stance cannot but convey a message to the reader that the teacher already knows what needs to be said. The teacher's role as mediator between pupils and poem is thus inadvertently reinforced. As such a role works consistently to undercut students' confidence in their own resources as readers, and as the school context itself reasserts such a role for the teacher, we need to provide as many opportunities as possible for pupils to assume full responsibility for making sense.

Anthologizing

One simple and direct way of counteracting such tendencies and reinforcing students' confidence in their own resources as readers of poetry is to have students choose the poems they wish to discuss. In this way, the teacher becomes a co-inquirer, who can genuinely be informed by students, rather than someone who already has all the answers.

Teachers can set up an appropriate situation for having students choose the works they wish to study. For instance, they can assign small groups of students the task of selecting from appropriate anthologies a set number of poems to become part of a class set to be studied in small groups. The choices may be built around particular themes, authors, periods, or forms. In all cases the students must ensure that the poems will be of general appeal to the class and present a challenge sufficient to warrant group effort. Thus each student might be expected to contribute two poems to the group's pool of appropriate poems. Members of the group will then choose from this pool the set number of poems as their contribution to the class anthology.

The procedure carries several benefits: the search for appropriate poems ensures that a great deal of poetry is read; paring the list down induces discussions that require pupils to choose, defend their choices, make judgments of the comparative worth and relevance of several poems, and thus arrive at some position on what they value and what they do not. The procedure allows, if properly managed, for a fair distribution of responsibility among members of the groups. Where such procedures have been tried, I am aware of several instances where individual members of groups generated (and illustrated) their own anthologies of poems they particularly liked in addition to the ones they contributed to the groups' final collections.

Skimming through several anthologies searching for appropriate poems demystifies for such readers the language of poetry. The more they read, the more likely are they to realize that the language of poetry is not as difficult as they had come to believe, requiring the intervention of a teacher to allow access to meaning. This process of familiarization is a vital step in any encounter between readers and language used in unfamiliar ways. It is the fact that poetry has been so mysterious that leads to readers' approaching a poem as if their task is "to crack the code." I am reminded here of an anecdote told by the late Canadian actor and director Maxim Mazumdar. During one of his regular in-school performance tours (a performance of *Macbeth*), he was approached by a sixteen-year-old girl who, quite moved by the performance and surprised how easily she had understood the performed text, was convinced that the actors had been using a "translation" and wondered where she could obtain such a version.

Preparing Readings

One of the more useful assignments in small-group work is to ask students to prepare readings or "performances" of particular poems. The readings may involve one or several readers, dramatization, the use of props, and musical accompaniment where appropriate. There are several advantages when all groups are working on the same poem. The onus is on each group to prepare a reading that can be justified to the other groups. There is strong incentive to devise a presentation that communicates their understanding, and there is a high level of interest in the presentations of the other groups. Discussion following the presentations can become quite animated.

There is also considerable benefit in the within-group discussions that precede presentation: the group must come to some consensus on their understanding of the poem and the kind of presentation that will best represent their understanding. Rehearsing the presentation will involve decisions about tone, inflection, pace, gesture, stance, and ways of representing or even highlighting some of the more interesting ambiguities in the text. In such discussions individual members of the group have the opportunity to exercise insight and intuition and to observe changing versions of the text as these emerge in the discussions. As they observe the presentations of the other groups, they come to realize the possibilities of meaning that the poem represents and their own stake in recovering such meanings. In the several readings that must precede such discussion the text becomes a familiar object. Moreover, the very nature of the task—interpretation and their sole responsibility for it—promotes the value of the personal knowledge and experience they bring to the task. Obviously, I am describing potential rather than ready achievement. The blocks to such achievement are again the very attitudes such activities are intended to overcome.

Writing Poetry

In the considerable discussion that has explored reading and writing relationships, an article by Frank Smith (1983), "Reading Like a Writer," is particularly valuable. It suggests that children must read like writers in order to write like writers; they must see themselves as authors. Readers of poetry may become better readers if they learn to read with a writer's (and in our case, a poet's) eye; that is, if they have joined what, following Smith, I would call the "club of poets." To join that community, they need to have tried their hand at writing poetry and to have been expected to write poetry.

It is interesting that most of us do not often ask or expect our students to write poetry because we believe that it is somehow beyond them, that their efforts will fall far short of what we generally regard as poetry. Yet we do not hesitate to ask them to write narratives or expository prose: in these modes we do not set up as a standard of acceptability what is published in a collection of short stories or essays. We keep our students out of the "club of poets" and make it difficult for them to read with a poet's eye, to read as a member of the club and therefore be willing to admire particularly apt phrasing or question what may seem strained or inappropriate. We may also consider how our own practice may have made poetry (reading and writing it) unlike stories and essays, marginal and even dilettantish; for some reason our students are not often encouraged to see links between the poems they read in schools and the advertising jingles and song lyrics that are so much a part of our culture.

Teaching About Poetry

This discussion thus far begs the question whether teachers have a role other than getting out of the way of the transaction between readers and poem. When and how does a teacher *teach* a poem? An answer to that question depends on how one defines teaching. I am sure I would be safe in assuming that generally teaching poetry has meant directing a process of reading in ways that ensure that students realize the experience that the poem, as understood by informed and experienced readers, is intended to represent. (I offer this definition on the basis of what I have seen is common practice in many classrooms.) That process of reading has invariably meant a process of guided questioning. This is precisely the role I have suggested teachers must shed if students are to become independent readers of poetry and to derive some enjoyment from a *personal* and *unmediated* act of interpretation. Of course, I am not dismissing the necessity for teachers to provide information that is vital to the understanding of a poem or information that might prevent certain misunderstanding. I would also recommend that initially students first meet the poem through the reading of the experienced reader, the teacher, but that as they grow in confidence as readers of poetry, they take increasing responsibility for presenting poems to the class. (Teachers should also encourage students to reread poems aloud, so that they become increasingly aware of the various ways in which poems appeal to the ear and sound evokes meaning.)

In suggesting that teachers attend primarily to creating productive contexts for the reading and discussion of poetry, I am not downplaying the importance of what one might call knowledge about poetry and the teacher's role in providing such information, be it information on poetic forms and devices or a particular literary movement. Generally such information has been provided *apart* from demands arising from the reading of a particular poem, and has been dispensed often as though it were a necessary preparation for the reading and study of a poem. Again, such practice has had the effect primarily of distancing students from their reading; there seemed to be no point in approaching a poem unless one had been prepared for that meeting by being given the right information. We are all familiar with poetry anthologies that do provide such information as an introduction, alerting readers in the hope of ensuring that they do not miss a single trick.

There is a fine line between information that directs one's response to a poem and information that enhances one's response. Rather than anticipate which is which, the teacher might rely more on requests for such information arising from the students' reading. The teacher ought to act prudently in meeting such requests. Are the students trying to find out "what the teacher wants"? At all costs, the teacher should avoid functioning as authorized reader with the authorized version of the poem. What matters is that the students have engaged the poem on their own terms (through small-group discussion, for instance) and that the need for particular information and the relevance of such information is immediately apparent. Not all questions need to be initiated by the students. In the small-group procedure I have described, for instance, some of the very questions a teacher feels a need to raise will come up in one or another individual group discussion. These questions will come as these readers become increasingly comfortable with poetic text, as they begin to notice differences in form and structure. Such openings into the formal and technical aspects of poetry cannot but arise when students give poems such concentrated attention. What I am insisting on is that attendance to technical matters should be the servant to engagement with poetry. Definitions of figures of speech do not matter to those who have not felt the force of a metaphor or been moved by a particular ordering of words.

I must emphasize that I am speaking generally of adolescent readers who do not trust themselves as readers of poetry and will readily yield to the teacher the right to make poems clear to them. Teachers need to consider these suggestions as part of a concerted program to help students recover their abilities as confident readers of poetry. And this program involves a phase of the teacher's patiently holding back her expert readings and expert knowledge until students are able to speak confidently from their own (and collectively developed, at the start) readings and to take teachers' responses under advisement, so to speak—"Let me think about that."

If this stance of not knowing and wanting to be informed (a stance the interviewer must hold during the RAP interviews) is difficult to adopt and maintain (it is not a matter of *pretending* not to know), we need to remind ourselves how difficult it is to persuade adolescents to our adult readings of certain television programs. Adolescent viewers, unlike most adolescent readers of poetry (and most literature, for that matter), feel quite confident about asserting and defending their versions of what they have seen on the screen. What should also give us pause in inserting prematurely our expert readings into a discussion is the realization that we can never again read a poem from a thirteen- or sixteen-year-old's point of view: we know too much, we have read many poems, and we have acquired considerable familiarity with a variety of genres of literature. We cannot help but regard as obvious and glaringly out there what is, for the adolescent reader, imperceptible or hardly worth making a fuss over.

Given these caveats, it is entirely appropriate in the post-small-group discussion phase for a teacher to wonder aloud about the choice of a particular word by the poet or to invite members of the class to reread a poem stressing a particular metrical feature or adopting a specific attitude on the speaker's part and wonder how such changes affect our response. My experience is that the small-group procedure almost always allows issues about diction, conventions, tradition, or technique to emerge as part of a relevant discussion of the poem. I recall a discussion among sixteen-year-olds of Shakespeare's Sonnet 130, "My mistress' eyes are nothing like the sun," soon moving, with only an encouraging nudge on my part ("Yes, let's talk about that"), into a discussion of exaggerated similes as a convention in poetry and some animated discussion on the use of simile, metaphor, and exaggeration in current poetry and in current usage in lyrics of love songs, greeting card verse, and advertising. Teachers need to weigh the need for providing what they believe is rele-

vant background information or information about certain conventions or
poetic devices against the likelihood that such interventions might reinforce
the notion that teachers have access to privileged information that unlocks
poems for them.

On the other hand, there is no need, especially in the postdiscussion
phase, for teachers to maintain a strictly neutral face and temper their enthusiasm or their dislike. Such a stance, however well meant, signals that the
teacher is somehow above it all. Because the students have dwelled for some
time on the poem and have had the opportunity to explore and develop their
responses through the talk of the small group, such contributions from the
teacher might come generally as a nudge to remain open to possibilities of
new meaning.

Choosing Poems

From the perspective of helping students become responsible and responsive
readers of poetry, the choice of poems we use becomes a key factor. I have
already mentioned why any induction into poetry ought to begin with a study
of contemporary poetry: so that students are not dependent on teachers to
explain unfamiliar vocabulary and references. It is also through contemporary
poetry that students will come to realize that their own experiences are relevant to uncovering the experiences presented in the poem.

The poems chosen also ought to justify their discussion within a small-
group format; that is, students ought to realize that the responses of others do
matter to their understanding, and that making sense of poetry is truly a collaborative enterprise. I believe small-group discussion is least productive
when the task set for the group does not in and of itself justify collaborative
effort and can be accomplished just as easily by individual members of the
group. Thus the poems used for group work ought to be sufficiently challenging to call forth a collective effort. Such effort over time soon makes clear to
participants that most poems of any significance reveal their several layers of
meaning and experience only after readers have considered multiple viewpoints and after several readings.

That said, it is also important to establish that not all poems need to be
discussed; that there are some poems that ought to be heard and reflected on
in silence. We need to demystify poetry; that is, we need to make poems familiar objects that can be picked up, read, put aside, and read again. One way
toward meeting such an agenda lies in establishing a poem-a-day program.
Students can be inducted into such a program by the teacher's daily reading of
a short poem she or he believes will engage the students. The poem can be presented on an overhead screen so that students both hear and see the poem yet
do not feel pressured to find a meaning. Such daily reading also induces
moments of quiet reflection that students come to value. Quite soon, students
can assume responsibility for choosing and reading the poem of the day.

Writing About Poetry

In my account of the design of this study I have already discussed the place of the poetry-response journal in recording one's response to a poem as that response has evolved from earlier discussion in the classroom. In suggesting such journals as a worthwhile activity, I wish to stress that they ought to be regarded as much more than a mere summation of the discussion that occurred in the classroom. When asking students to write in response to a rereading of the poem some time later at home, I remind them that it is quite likely that their response to the poem may have altered. Their appreciation of the poem may have grown, decreased, or stayed the same; they may have made newer connections with their past experience and with other readings. I hope through these rereadings that they come to think of poems as dynamic entities whose meaning is set for all time by any particular reading. Early in such projects, their journal entries are usually short, generally a summation of what they recall from the day's discussion; however, four or five such sessions later, they tend to write longer entries, which are far more reflective in mode.

I respond daily to these journals. I avoid any hint of confirming or not confirming the readings; I merely wish to establish that I am curious about their responses and that I have read them with interest. Thus I express delight or pleasant surprise, seek clarification, wonder about the source of a particular observation, mention someone else's response, or suggest a poem they might find interesting and sometimes insert a copy of that poem—in short, I respond as an interested listener.

I have also provided a brief description of the stream-of-consciousness response procedure. Such stream-of-consciousness accounts can be used as the basis from which small-group discussion proceeds. In both journal responses and stream-of-consciousness responses, writing is used as a means of retrieving, recording, and reordering one's response. Writing can also be used to record and report on the outcome of small-group discussion. A more formal writing task would involve asking students to choose one of the poems they have already discussed on a particular theme and discuss why that poem is a particularly apt choice to be included in a collection of poems on that theme.

Teachers might also experiment with having students write poems in imitation of poems they have just read. Such writing requires that students work out the formal features and style of that poem so that they can imitate it. They may choose to parody the poem or use the particular form and style to work on their own topic. In tasks that involve imitation, it is best for them to begin by working collaboratively in small groups before undertaking any such work independently.

I offer these suggestions as examples of writing tasks that begin in the reader's response and work primarily to enhance that response rather than attempt to satisfy a model response that may exist in a teacher's head. I am sure readers can come up with several other suggestions that respect these guidelines.

Additional Resources

In suggesting these approaches to poetry in school, I have been concerned first to establish a classroom climate that allows students to move away from their dependence on the teacher as interpreter and to develop a confidence in their ability to make sense of poetry on their own. Second, I have suggested contexts that allow students to function as successful readers despite any differences in the ways they go about reading a poem. I have refrained therefore from suggesting approaches that place the teacher at the center of the reading, for instance, as one who uses certain introductory exercises to create in the students a mental set appropriate to the reception of the poem. However worthwhile, such activities inadvertently remind students that the reading of poetry, unlike the reading of a short story or a novel, must be mediated by the teacher. Such activities, I believe, may have their place once students approach a poem with the same confidence in their resources as readers as they display when they pick up a work of fiction they have chosen to read. Keeping these qualifications in mind, I suggest in the Bibliography some resources for additional ideas on teaching poetry reading and writing.

In the discussion that follows I consider the question of whether and how teachers may intervene to influence a reader's way of making sense of poetry.

Patterns of Reading and Teacher Intervention

Spiro (1982, 55) points out how information-processing models have created a climate favoring mechanistic models and stressing reading efficiency at all costs. The patterns of reading I have described are likely to induce teachers to abstract those strategies that appear productive and to teach these strategies. Should we not, in helping readers like Pierre, teach problem-solving strategies that would turn such readers away from their trial-and-error approach toward approaches that do not shunt intractable information aside and do encourage the tentative consideration of several possible meanings rather than the easy adoption of the first rough fit? Such an approach treats symptoms rather than causes. Spiro (1979) makes a similar point in an article dealing with differences in comprehension styles. The danger here is that reading poetry may become mechanical and merely the application of techniques for comprehending rather than for evoking and apprehending the poem.

Teaching explicit comprehension strategies rather than creating the contexts within which reading for meaning can become functional may explain why, according to the National Assessment of Educational Progress (1981), the students in the survey had by and large learned to read a wide variety of material but were generally unable to account for their understandings by returning to the text to examine and analyze. The NAEP study suggests a general inability to do so; however, the transcripts of the small-group work and the RAPs in my study demonstrate that most pupils will turn to the text to support their meanings because the context demands it. Teaching comprehension strategies decontextualizes reading and produces results that are not necessarily reflected in reading outside the teaching situation. In her study of good and poor readers of short stories, Weisberg (1979) found that both good and poor readers were able to answer specific questions probing for implicit information, but that such implicit information was not found in their "free recall" protocols. This suggests that most teaching discourages readers' taking responsibility for making meaning, unless such making is specifically negotiated by questions.

For these reasons, I would say, intervening to reorient an individual's pattern of reading seems unwarranted. If these patterns of reading, as I believe, are directed powerfully by the expectations brought to the reading, by readers' attitudes and stances toward poetic text, and if these expectations, stances, and attitudes have much to do with the contexts within which poetry is taught and read, then we need to consider how those contexts (the causes) can be modified.

Patterns of reading will shift over time, most likely, in contexts that provide practice at the task, opportunities to try out, modify, and confirm perceptions and hunches. Small-group work of the kind I have described provides such opportunities. It allows students to take charge of their own reading, to try out possibilities of meaning, and reinforces the notion of reading as a transaction between reader and text, a process of continually negotiating meaning. Over a year after the commencement of this study, I returned to the school to collect additional RAPs from ten of the fourteen original participants. I used a different set of poems. The individual RAP sessions were preceded by two small-group discussion sessions to induct students once more into the process of reading and talking about poems. My hypothesis was that some slight shifts might have occurred in individuals' patterns of reading poetry.

If there had been shifts, they were hard to detect in the RAP transcripts. The characteristic patterns were still there; some RAPs could even be correctly assigned to their authors by reviewers familiar with the students' individual reading patterns. If there had been no noticeable changes in patterns, must we assume that fifteen months is not enough time for any such changes to have occurred? Or should I infer that these patterns of reading are much more set in individual ways of behaving than I expected and are consequently hard to shift? The explanation for the absence of any noticeable change in patterns may be much simpler. Over fifteen months between the collection of the two sets of RAPs very little poetry had been read, and when taught, had been presented within a teacher-directed format. None of the pupils had been involved in small-group discussion of poetry sessions for any length of time that might allow for changes in patterns of reading. None of the students reported that any similar small-group discussion of texts had gone on in any concerted fashion in other subject areas. Maturational factors, in and of themselves, had obviously not occasioned a noticeable shift; hence, these readers, when invited to read poetry freely again, responded in the ways they had fifteen months earlier. Whether regular undirected small-group discussion of poetry might have helped modify patterns of reading remains a moot point. All readers, however, did say they continued to read poetry with a growing sense of confidence in their ability to make sense of it.

The RAP as a Teaching and Diagnostic Tool

Teachers may see in the RAP procedure a means of learning more about how their students read poetry. One way of getting around the problem of scheduling the large number of interviews involved would be to invite students to record their RAPs privately, or better still, with the aid of a fellow student as conversational partner. And, of course, the RAPs need not be transcribed. The success of the private RAP procedure will depend very much on the kind of work that has preceded the sessions and on whether the students have acquired the confidence to think aloud and at length as they attempt to make sense of a poem.

The RAP procedure can also be a means of helping students understand their own processes as readers of poetry. If teachers act as interviewers, they might at the conclusion of the RAP session ask students to reflect on the process they have just gone through and say how they think they go about making sense of a poem. Subsequent discussion, individual or class, can focus on some of the moves they have identified and the extent to which they regard them as productive or unproductive.

As I said earlier, students differ in their awareness of how they read a poem. Problem solvers tend to monitor their own process of making meaning during the RAPs, and when they are asked to recall the process, provide accounts that reflect the process fairly well. Such self-reflective understanding (what cognitive psychologists refer to as metacognitive awareness) is a major step in helping students take charge of their own reading. I provide here a description by Rick, the fourteen-year-old English reader I cited earlier, of how he goes about making sense of a poem. He uses as an example a poem he has just been discussing in a RAP interview:

> What I do, I get an idea and put that to one side, and another, I put that aside, and then I draw a line between "the stone house" with "the den," and then I'll move them into the middle and I'll have "stone house," "den," and I'd do another one like "thoughts" to "clinging apples," bring that in the middle. [All along, Rick is moving his hand over the surface of the desk in front of him, sketching how and where on some imagined surface he arranges his ideas.] Now I've got "stone," "den," "thoughts etc.," and "little apples." I keep doing that until I build up a pattern. There are still some

ideas scattered around the outside, and then when you [the interviewer] read it through [aloud, during the session], I tick off the ideas saying, "That's OK, that's OK." Then maybe one is wrong, and I'll throw it out; that goes back to the outside and I try and fit another idea in from the ones that are scattered around the outside.

[Interviewer: Do they all fit in?]

No. Some of them are scattered around the outside, and if the idea doesn't fit, you [I] read them through and that goes to one side again, and another is tried and another, and another, until it sort of all matches up [and on for another ten lines].

Rick's awareness of his own processes as a reader is impressive by any standard. I would argue that this awareness has developed through the small-group discussion and has grown sharper through the RAP interviews.

Further Research

This study sought to determine what occurs when adolescent readers go about making sense of a poem. Clearly, an exploratory study of this kind must be viewed with some caution. Much work remains to be done before some of the central questions raised in this book can be answered.

In the first place, the study needs to be replicated with a much larger number of students so that the methodology used in this study can be tested by other researchers, and the proposed patterns of reading and the elements that chart these patterns can be validated. That expansion of the study may well include adolescent readers in other English-speaking countries so that the links between individuals' patterns of reading and their cultural backgrounds can be explored.[2] The methodology needs to be tested as well with a view to establishing whether RAPs can be obtained without the presence of the interviewer.[3] Clearly, the interviewer's presence and reactions can considerably influence the outcome of the RAP sessions. Adult readers are more likely than adolescents to be able to proceed without the presence of an interviewer to urge them to say what they are thinking.

There is a need as well to consider several case studies that would track the development of reading patterns over a number of years and examine the relations among these patterns and several aspects of the individuals' backgrounds. One would also need to know how particular teaching practices influence the patterns of reading. While there is no reason to believe that the choice of poem makes a significant difference to the pattern of responding, the poems certainly need to be chosen with that particular consideration in mind. It would be interesting as well to adapt the methodology in order to

2. I have conducted such a study and it is scheduled for publication in the near future.
3. Several teachers have experimented with such an approach; however, the results are mixed. Some students need the urging of a supportive listener if they are to persist with second and third readings.

obtain responses to short fiction[4] so that comparisons between patterns of reading poetry and reading fiction can be made. Vipond and Hunt's (1984) identification of three strategies in the reading of fiction, for instance, provides interesting parallels to the patterns I have proposed.

To Conclude

One of the main reasons for this study was to test a methodology for tapping response to poetry as that response occurs. I am convinced that RAPs provide rich data on the processes by which readers come to an understanding of a poem. I cannot emphasize enough that there is more to those processes than is reported in the RAPs. Moreover, despite considerable effort to reduce the effect of the context in which the RAPs are obtained, one must understand that some readers may find the RAP context more amenable than others; others will have been "more themselves" in the small-group situation. Still others may have revealed much more about their reading processes in the writing they have done in their journals. All this argues for a more careful assembling of supplementary data and an equally careful consideration of such data.

For these reasons, and because of the size of the sample, I have advanced this account of patterns in the process of reading and responding to poetry with some degree of tentativeness. I will insist, however, that there are significant differences among readers in the ways they go about reading and responding to poetry, that these differences can be described, and that the expectations and attitudes that powerfully influence such patterns of reading and responding are engendered largely by teacher-dominated practices that prevail in the teaching of poetry. This study will have made a difference if it leads teachers to seriously reconsider those practices.

4. Asking readers to respond aloud as they read a story is a far more disruptive intervention than is such a request when they are reading a poem. Readers of stories are involved, for example, in an automatized (by now) process of constructing the story; that is, weaving a thread of narrative, placing events in that thread, recalling and recasting past events in the light of current developments, inferring character and predicting outcomes, and so on. Students invited to comment when they want to, as they read, choose the moments when they feel they can step out of the story to report on their developing response, or opt to comment after they have finished reading. In that case they flip back through the story, recalling their responses and reflections as they go along. Rather than responding as they read, they are recalling how they responded and responding to those responses.

Afterword

Poetry still remains a neglected area of study in both elementary and secondary schools, largely, I believe, on account of a perceived antipathy to poetry among adolescent students and a corresponding reluctance among teachers to include more than a token amount of poetry in their programs. In elementary schools the focus for too long has been on teaching reading comprehension rather than cultivating a delight in poetry for its own sake. Although that focus is now shifting, far too many teachers confess considerable uncertainty about their own ability to read and respond to poetry, an uncertainty that corresponds (when they must teach poetry) with a dependence on textbook questions and guides and a lack of confidence that students can arrive at worthwhile responses without considerable direction on the teacher's part.

Of all literary genres, it seems to me, poetry remains very much a school genre: something that is read and taught only within classrooms and unlikely to be picked up and read outside a classroom. Somewhere between the early childhood joy in nursery rhymes and the antipathy to and fear of poetry one finds in the adolescent years lies the teacher question, "What does this poem mean?" and the expectation of one right answer. It is somewhat disconcerting that some recent literature textbook series, while they profess a reader-response-oriented approach, still display in the series of questions that follow a poem or a story a tendency to guide responses toward preferred readings.

Louise Rosenblatt (1938; 1978) has waged a long uphill battle to displace the tyranny of the text and the authorized meaning with the notion of the poem as a transaction between reader, text, and context. The battle seems to have been won, with teachers turning increasingly to "real" stories, poems, and books and away from soulless constructed simulations, with teachers moving away from the head and center of the classroom as mediators of meaning to the sidelines as supporters and co-inquirers assigning to students the right to develop and explore their own understandings, and finally, with teachers recognizing the central place of affect in literary reading and enabling the expression of feeling and readers' connections with personal experience.

But with all this emphasis on personal response, teachers also know that they walk an uneasy tightrope between a commonplace misrepresentation of response-centered teaching as "a poem or a story is *whatever* you want it to mean" and the widely held notion that meaning is resident entirely in the text and teachers must function as guardians of authorized readings. In between lies Rosenblatt's (1978) commonsensical argument that no one else can read a poem or a story for us as well as all that such a reminder implies for classroom practice:

- Classrooms afford students unique opportunities to exchange readings and revise and expand their own in the light of what they hear from readers like themselves.

- In such transactions the text they have read in common is both an invitation to explore and a constraint.

- Students' personal experiences, including those derived from their reading, provide the basis from which they can question and assess what is being offered by the text.

That such teaching is so easily misconstrued by the larger public is evidenced by a well-orchestrated negative reaction to a commendable attempt in California's English-Language Arts Assessment proposal to legitimize affect in literary reading by asking students to talk about their feelings as part of their response to a literary text. We need to plan carefully against such regressive misreadings. The case for programs that value and nurture readers, especially the marginalized, will be made largely through successful demonstrations rather than by argument. I hope this book goes some way toward achieving those demonstrations.

Appendix A

Poems Used in the Study

Pre-test[1]

William Stafford, "Fifteen"

Procedure-Modeling Sessions—Poems About Poetry (Whole Class)

Eve Merriam, "How to Eat a Poem"

John Moffitt, "To Look at Anything"

Naoshi Koriyama, "Unfolding Bud"

Practice Session (Small Group)

Theodore Roethke, "My Papa's Waltz"

Robert Frost, "Fire and Ice"

Sessions 1–10

Irving Layton, "The Bull-Calf"

Seamus Heaney, "The Early Purges"

Alden Nowlan, "The Bull Moose"

Stevie Smith, "The Best Beast at the Fat-Stock Show at Earl's Court"

---

1. The pre-test was intended primarily to help confirm the makeup of the target group. A post-test did not figure in the design.

Alden Nowlan, "The First Stirring of the Beasts"

Charles Causley, "Green Man in the Garden"

A. J. M. Smith, "The Lonely Land"

Ted Hughes, "Wind"

Seamus Heaney, "Follower"

Dale Zieroth, "Father"

Responding-Aloud Protocol Sessions

Session 1

Robert Graves, "Warning to Children," or

Margaret Atwood, "Cyclops"

Session 2

Al Purdy, "Detail," or

Seamus Heaney, "Blackberry-Picking"

(Half the pupils chosen for the RAP sessions read a Canadian poem in the first session and a British poem in the second. The other half did the reverse.)

Stream-of-Consciousness Protocol Sessions (Whole Class)

Sylvia Plath, "Mushrooms"

Margaret Atwood, "Dreams of the Animals"

Appendix B

Responding-Aloud Protocols: "Cyclops"

Cyclops

You, going along the path,
mosquito-doped, with no moon, the flashlight
a single orange eye

unable to see what is beyond
the capsule of your dim   5
sight, what shape

contracts to a heart
with terror, bumps
among the leaves, what makes
a bristling noise like a fur throat   10

Is it true you do not wish to hurt them?

Is it true you have no fear?
Take off your shoes, then,
let your eyes go bare,
swim in their darkness as in a river   15

do not disguise
yourself in armour

They watch you from hiding;
you are a chemical
smell, a cold fire, you are   20
giant and indefinable

In their monstrous night
thick with possible claws
where danger is not knowing,

you are the hugest monster.   25

Angie

Interviewer (after the poem is read): Any questions?

Angie: (*laughs*) No, eh . . .

Any words that bother you, or . . . ?

Well, . . . when it says "unable to see what is beyond / the capsule" . . .
what they mean by . . .

A capsule is, um, is . . . you remember what the capsule for the rockets
look like on the top of the spaceship, you know, the astronauts in a capsule, sort of like that shape. Or a capsule, like a capsule for pills
. . . you know, it's sort of like that, eh?

Ya.

Ya. So it's that kind of shape.

(*long pause*)[1]

Any other word?

I don't think so. Ah, it's so different, I'm so used to doing in a group
and . . .

Ya. Okay, well, just . . . you know, what are your . . . sort of your immediate, your first reactions to the poem. There's no right or wrong, so just
take a shot.

Well I don't see how cyclops is joined with the chemical. . . with the
poem. That's what I'm trying to . . . 'cause the way it is, like, at the
beginning it looks as if he's, like, in the forest going, and it's dark, and
his flashlight going through, trying to find something, but . . .

You know what cyclops is?

Isn't it an ancient god, like, Greek god or something?

It's um, . . . it's a monster, a giant, with one eye.

(pause) Oh, so I guess they're just comparing you to this thing, the
cyclops, like the way . . . the way they're describing it with the flashlight, like the flashlight is your eye. Like that's the only thing that's

1. (*unclear*) indicates undecipherable speech. Pauses of different durations are represented as follows: . . . (less than five seconds); *pause, long pause, v. long pause* (five seconds to one minute);
pause, __ sec. (over one minute). It was during the longer pauses that the interviewer would
remind readers to say what they were thinking.

giving you vision. I—so I guess they're describing it to the cyclops. Um . . .

Why don't you read the poem to yourself? Okay? It sometimes helps.

Yes. (*v. long pause*) Still, I think this is a (*unclear*) going around and the way they're describing it, like . . . with possible claws, like you have weapons. And like the animals are just going around, they all see you, like, they're in hiding. And you're with the flashlight going around with one eye trying to find them and . . . the way, like . . . "do not disguise / yourself in armour" (*v. long pause*) 'cause I guess, like, they scent you, like, they smell you—the chemicals smell cold (*long pause*) And consider . . . like . . . describing them, like . . . comparing with the animals, like, they, no . . . like, they have, like, a defense but not against you; like, they have a weapon or something, that's why they . . . they reconsider you as the hugest monster. Uh . . . (*long pause*)

Then they say "Is it true you have no fear?" like, are you so brave that you can come in and just shoot anyone and . . . like . . . if you . . . (*pause*) and then they say, oh then, okay, take off your shoes, show us, like, you know, but you don't have to . . . come in with this weapon, like, why do you need the weapon to make yourself so . . . fearless and all this, like, take away the weapon, take away all your defenses and. . . see how . . . brave you are and all this. (*v. long pause*) It's, like, if . . . cyclops—no, I don't . . . (*pause*) 'cause I guess this was monstrous . . . like, no one was . . . like, he wasn't afraid of anyone, the cyclops probably; he was . . . was a one-eyed vision going around and . . . this, you had a . . . person in a . . . probably in a forest going, he has this . . . flashlight like the cyclops, like one eye going, like . . . they . . . with the . . . like, that's, like, what the flashlight shows you is what you see only. Um . . . (*v. long pause*) Well, that's about it, like. (*pause*)

Read it aloud, okay.

Oh (*laughs*) I don't . . . okay. (*reads entire poem*)

Just read the last four lines again.

(*reads last four lines again*)

Right. I just wanted to point that it's *their*.

Okay.

Okay. Any other responses or thoughts or feelings or . . . anything at all?

(*v. long pause*)

Try to tell me what you're thinking about.

Well, the last part, I guess, like, it's . . . where they live, in the forest, I guess, or whatever, there is a danger but not (*unclear*), you know, you gotta watch what's going on, like, in the forest. I guess they did what they want, and . . . "in their monstrous night," I guess that was caused by this man walking around with this light . . . and I guess they can't see him; he can only see them with the flashlight, and he's the hugest monster because . . . he has . . . the power over them at that point. And . . . and he had the possible claws, like he has probably some weapons, like, you know, that he can use on them. (*v. long pause*) And I guess, like, after they say like, listen, if you . . . if you lived there you'd know, but now you come in your armour and you come and you don't . . . you try to . . . you try to act like the cyclops or whatever, you know? (*v. long pause*) That's about it, like. (*v. long pause*)

Anything else that occurs to you or goes through your mind?

No, not really, it's just . . . it seems so easy that, like, uh, it seems that I'm missing something 'cause it seems so easy, like, just . . . this guy's walking on a path with a flashlight trying to find something, and . . . he's acting so brave and all this but . . . the only thing that's in my head is this werewolf thing 'cause I saw the movie at lunch. (*both laugh*) It's the only thing that's coming into my head now.

Tell me this, then, Angie: how does the poem make you feel?

(v. long pause) I find, like, this . . . poem is trying to give . . . I don't know. The animals are trying to . . . give their impression of hunters or something like . . . trying to . . . say, like, you men, you try and act so big, or something.

Does it make you feel any particular kind of way?

Well, more or less, I'd be on the animals' side 'cause, like, me, I'm not ag—I'm . . . against these hunting things, like . . . 'cause it's . . . it's true, like, the animals have no defense, like, they just live, and they have to run around, and these guys run with guns and . . . you know. And then they take up, you know, the lives of . . . the animals and—(*long pause*)

Anything else you want to add? You want to read it one more time or anything, and see if there's anything you'd like to add?

I doubt it. I'll read it afterwards. I'm gonna (*laughs*) it's gonna bug me, like, after, when I'll probably find something. Not now. (*v. long pause*) I, like, it seems as if he already, like, found some animals 'cause he hears them among the leaves. With the noise and all that. (*long pause*)

Okay? Okay, thanks very much, Angie.

Pierre

Interviewer (*after the poem is read*): Any questions about vocabulary? Any words you don't understand?

Pierre: I don't think so.

No?

(*unclear*)

Okay. Any initial response? Any feeling, anything that happens to you as you—

> I don't know, all this, eh, you—you—you there, like, eh . . . gives me a—g—some kind of an urge to figure out, like, who it is, you is like, eh, what it is, here. That's, eh . . . that's about it. It got me curious.

Uh-huh? Anything else?

> (*pause*) (*unclear*)

Okay, well, why don't you read it to yourself silently, and if at any time during it you have anything to say, while you're reading it to yourself, just say it; if not, wait until you finish.

> (*pause, 90 sec.*) (*reads silently*) I don't know, like, eh, this, eh, meaning doesn't make sense but . . . somehow I got . . . God in here . . . "you are a chemical / smell, a cold fire, you are" a giant and undefinable, this . . . just this part here means (*unclear*) God.

M-hmm.

> . . . but really, like, I don't think God is really . . . has anything to do with fear (*pause*) or hurting. (*pause*) That's what I got. (*v. long pause*) I think it's the "single orange eye" there, the flashlight, "a single orange eye." (*pause, 90 sec.*)

Say—try to say everything that you're thinking, everything that occurs to you or goes through your mind.

> (*v. long pause*)

Nothing? Anything that makes you feel, or any kind of response you want to make?

> (*v. long pause*)

Why don't you read it out loud, then?

> (*reads entire poem without comment*) (*long pause*)

Any thoughts or feelings or responses to that?

> (*hesitation*)

It can't be wrong, don't worry about it, so just take a shot. Anything that—does it make you feel anything?

> (*quietly*) Can't really say if I *feel* anything but—(*v. long pause*)

Try telling me what you're thinking about while you're reading it.

> (*unclear*) There's something, a dream or something . . . people are looking in? (*unclear*) This cave, I guess, and, uh . . . maybe he's hiding back there 'cause maybe this . . . well, s—well, let's say cyclops isn't really . . . this, eh . . . dangerous or . . . he says "do not disguise / yourself in armour" so maybe there's nothing really to be afraid of under the armour?

M-hmm.

(*unclear*) (*v. long pause*) What's a "fur throat"?

Um . . . I don't know, I don't think that, um . . . I think it's just like a . . . an animal throat.

Okay. (*v. long pause*)

Try to keep talking about what you're thinking about.

Well, like, here I get, like, eh . . . in this, uh . . . person . . . the only, really cyclops person's been taken by a disease or something and eh . . . and eh, the really, the . . . it's the person himself like saying, like, eh . . . "swim in their darkness as in a river" like "swim in their darkness" meaning, eh . . . this person here, like, their life is like darkness so try . . . try to understand how this person is? and do not disguise yourself normally means, um . . . (*unclear*) person gets all dressed up, like, so nobody can really see how . . . person really is? (*v. long pause*)

I'll read it again, okay? Maybe you just listen to me reading it again. (*reads entire poem again*) What do you think? Any responses? feelings?

I'm not . . . no, I'm not even (*unclear*) by that. (*v. long pause*)

Try to keep in touch with what you're thinking about. Let me know.

I keep reading it and reading and reading it, ya.

M-hmm. (*long pause*). What—what—what part of the poem caused you any sort of problem, do you think?

Well I (*unclear*) looking at the last part . . . and I can't really . . . get it, so I (*unclear*) go back to the first part and I keep reading it and reading it. (*v. long pause*) I'm trying to figure who would those animals be . . . eh . . . "Is it true you do not wish to hurt them?" (*v. long pause*)

What do you—who do you think it is?

I'm not sure yet, so that's why I keep reading it.

Ya.

—find something. (*v. long pause*)

Who's "you"?

(*unclear*) The, eh . . . subject of the poem?

M-hmm . . . and who is that?

(*v. long pause*)

No thoughts on that?

No.

Okay, read it again, with this in mind: "You, going along the path," the person walking along the path with a flashlight . . . okay? Read it again with that in mind. It's about a person walking along a path with a flashlight in their hand.

(*v. long pause*) Well, here, like, ah . . . I felt, like, okay, the person is, he's walking with a flashlight—

M-hmm?

And, eh . . . to these . . . let's say animals or bugs, like, we're . . . we're so big, like . . . and, eh, we're monsters to them, like, we're their cyclops . . . like, and, eh . . . the flashlight, like, probably doesn't flash very far, so, like, eh . . . all around you can't really see what really's happening . . . so that's why, eh . . . your heart, like, is, eh . . . with terror then so you're just wondering what's gonna . . . come next as you keep going along . . . (*long pause*) . . . and, like, eh . . . when the person, like, is going through the woods or something; most people aren't going to be there to hurt the animals unless they're hunting or . . . so that's why I guess it says here "Is it true you do not wish to hurt them?" You're just out there with a flashlight? (*v. long pause*) . . . So "swim in their darkness" is probably, eh . . . eh . . . search, eh . . . the woods (*unclear*) the path—search the path around you? Like, not the . . . darkness (*unclear*) 'cause I'm . . . ah, here "They watch you from hiding; / you are a chemical / smell" . . . so, like, eh . . . animals can pick up, like, your smell, like from the air, I think? (*v. long pause*) Maybe this *is* hunting (*unclear*) . . . you know? "In their monstrous night / thick with possible claws" maybe claws is a weapon? a gun? or . . . "where danger is not knowing" . . . when they don't really know what the danger is? . . . from these claws? And "you are the hugest monster" so . . . the person . . . along the path is, eh . . . big? (*v. long pause*)

Anything else? Anything you'd like to add to that?

(*v. long pause*)

Try to let me know what you're thinking about.

Makes me think, like, I, sometimes I . . . well, I used to . . . I used to go to the woods a lot . . . and I sort of . . . put myself in his position and try to see what . . . what it's like walking through the woods, like (*pause*) I know a few times I've been in the woods (*unclear*) [at] night and . . . I've got a great amount of fear 'cause I can't really see . . . what's around me. Just the trees. So I'm trying to put myself in this person's place, going along the path.

M-hmm. How does it make you feel? Since you've had that memory?

A little fearful (*unclear*) (*v. long pause*)

Anything you'd like to add to that?

(*v. long pause*)

Okay, one last question. Why do you think that, um, at first you couldn't figure out, you know, when you first read it, you couldn't figure out what was happening. What—what—what do you think threw you off, made it difficult for you to figure it out?

It was the, eh, title.

The title.

> Right. (*unclear*) . . . it says "Cyclops" here at the . . . beginning, and
> then when you start reading it . . . that's all that's really in my mind so
> that . . . sort of blocks me off from . . . searching (*unclear*) . . . and
> then . . . after a while . . . from just reading it and reading it this sort of
> fades off and . . . get involved in the poem.

Okay, you want to make any last statement about it, or—do you like the
poem?

> Ya, it's interesting (*unclear*) (*v. long pause*) I wish I could get more out
> of it because, eh . . . (*v. long pause*) 'cause here he's making state-
> ments and then he just sort of leaves it there blank . . . sort of getting
> you to think about it, I guess.

M-hmm? (*long pause*) Well, having been in the woods at night, does it
. . . what more comes to you, what more—is there more of a feeling that
you get from it? You said fearful.

> Yeah.

Anything else?

> (*v. long pause*) (*unclear*) and, like, eh . . . like, it's so empty like, eh
> (*unclear*) there and it's like, eh (*unclear*) I think here, eh (*unclear*)
> empty. . . right here, right now.

Ya.

> (*v. long pause*) Like, "a cold fire." Fire is warm . . . but fire presents
> danger, so maybe you are not . . . danger that's like a cold fire? (*v. long
> pause*)

Remember, this—they watch from hiding and what do they see?

> (*v. long pause*)

Anything else you want to add?

> (*v. long pause*) "you are a chemical" Maybe . . . because of the way we
> live? (*unclear*) today, like, eh, we need so many . . . chemicals
> (*unclear*) That's what I think why it says "you are a chemical." I mean,
> "smell" is completely . . . by itself after it starts off "smell."

Ya.

> And it's sort of presumed (*unclear*)

Ya.

> (*v. long pause*)

Remember you started off, you were talking about—saying that there was
a feeling about God in there, do you want to . . . go back to that?

> (*long pause*) Well, I got that 'cause, like, "indefinable" (*unclear*)
> "indefinable" . . . usually (*unclear*) . . . big things like, eh . . . [easy to

find? easy to define?] or . . . "you are / giant and indefinable" . . . something or can't . . . see it, I guess; darkness . . . darkness is big, but you can't . . . sort of find it, you can't see (*unclear*).

Okay, is there anything else you want to add?

(*unclear*)

Okay. Thanks very much.

Petra

Interviewer: This is called "Cyclops."

Petra: I don't know what that is. (*laughs*)

Okay. Um, cyclops is a figure from Greek mythology; it's a big giant who had one eye. It's from the story of Odysseus, or Ulysses as he is called sometimes, and, eh, it's just a great big giant with one eye.

Okay.

Okay? (*reads poem*) Comments?

Okay. Um, I think that, ah, there's lots of, um . . . there's lone—a certain loneliness . . . if you're the—okay, I think that you're the—the monster, you're the, um . . . the cyclops? Is that what it is? Okay.

Cyclops?

Yeah. And um, I think that you, okay . . . you're the giant, you're in control, you know you're—you know you're the one that's, ah . . . you know no fear, that sort of thing, um, but there is a certain loneliness to it because you're all alone in the woods, um, you know, it's so dark and . . . that's about it.

Okay. Um, any questions about vocabulary or anything like that?

Um, let me see . . . okay, "capsule of your dim."

Let's see, um, "capsule of your dim sight"?

Yeah.

Ah . . . capsule is like a Tylenol capsule, it just means something that's . . . ya, like tunnel, I guess, would be a good synonym.

Um. (*pause*). I guess that's about it.

Okay. If there are any more questions, you can just ask them as you go along.

Okay.

Do you want to read it silently all the way through?

Ya.

Okay.

(*reads silently*)

Okay?

I'm ready.

Any more comments about—

> Um . . . I think that . . . whoever wrote this poem is asking, "Are you
> the . . . are you the monster?" as if saying, "Are you . . . not scared to
> do things?" and it's like a simile to . . . comparing you to . . . a monster
> and to yourself. As if saying like, are you—would you do stuff on your
> own, would you—are you afraid to do things? and if you aren't, then
> take off your shoes and go, go ahead and do it, you know?

Okay. Um, do you want to go . . . now?

> You mean by . . . stanza by stanza?

Ya. Go, sort of stanza by stanza?

> Okay. (reads lines 1–3) (unclear)

Wherever it's comfortable for you to stop.

> Okay. Okay. "You, going along the path, mosquito-doped." Okay, I
> think that's, ah, you're walking along . . . along the path. I think that—
> that shows you're walking along your life . . . you know, stages of life,
> mosquito-doped; mosquitoes all around you?

That could be. Um. somebody asked me in the other class, and I think we
used to say when I was a little child, if I remember correctly, that to put
mosquito-dope was literally repellent for mosquitoes. You put on a liquid
that keeps them away.

> Okay, that might mean that, okay, while you're . . . while you're . . .
> going along in life, mosquito-doped, okay, um . . . shielded by other
> people, . . . okay, like, ah, you—there's always warnings not to hitch-
> hike or things like that, that might be it, I think. Okay, with no moon,
> that might mean, ah, you have no—okay there's "no moon, / the flash-
> light a single orange eye / unable to see what is beyond / the capsule of
> your dim / sight," okay, um . . . with no moon, no guiding light, just
> the flashlight, just, you know, a certain . . . amount of . . . safety or
> whatever. "single orange eye / unable to see what is beyond / the cap-
> sule of your dim / sight," um . . . maybe you're not . . . you're not sure
> what is . . . what is ahead of you, and all you have is this little light,
> showing you, you know, it's take one day at a time, something like
> that. Okay, "what shape / contracts to a heart / with terror," that I don't
> get. (whispers) "what shape / contracts to a heart." (pause) Um . . .
> could it mean that, um . . . what—what you experience might, you
> know, might shake you up, or whatever? I'm not sure (unclear)
> "bumps / among," "bumps / among the leaves, what makes / a bristling
> noise like a fur throat." Okay, that mea--I guess that means . . . what-
> ever is behind the trees or, you know, hiding there, you don't know
> what it is, and you just hear noise. That might be, like, in life, if you
> don't know what's ahead of you, and you hear something like a certain

warning or whatever . . . that's all okay. "Is it true you do not wish to hurt them?" Oh God. Um . . . you—I guess that means you don't want to hurt . . . you want—you want to be careful what you do in your life . . . I'm not sure.

"Is it true you have no fear?" Okay . . . um . . . well, that says it: if you have no fear, okay go ahead then, experience, and if you . . . you know, if you trust yourself . . . "let your eyes go bare, / swim in their darkness as [in] a river" . . . Okay. "swim in the darkness as in a river" Okay, that means that . . . ah . . . it's, like, search around you, experience just, you know, if you trust yourself, do like a river, spread yourself out and you know. Okay, "do not disguise / yourself in armour." Ah, don't be fake. Don't, don't try to show yourself off because you're afraid of experiencing. "They watch you from hiding" that must be other people, I guess. "you are a chemical," ah, "a chemical / smell, a cold fire, you are / giant and undefinable." Okay. You're yourself, if—if you are . . . the giant, if you have no fear . . . then you—you're in control, you can . . . you know, say. . . whatever you feel, whatever. "In the[ir] monstrous night / thick with possible claws where danger is not knowing." That means . . . um . . . there might be danger ahead but you know it's there, but, um . . . you know that . . . you can control it if you're . . . so big. "you are the hugest monster." You're in control.

Okay. Now, that's . . . very interesting, and, um . . . but I must have misheard something at the beginning. When—when I read it through the first time, do you remember what you said to me right afterwards? About what you thought that—

I think I said . . . oh God, I forget. Ah, what did I say my first impression. Um . . . I guess what I said was that . . . the author is using you as a—a synonym to the, um, to the giant. I'm not sure I think that's what it was.

Okay, it's just that I thought you had, um, come up with two different ideas there. I couldn't remember.

I think I did . . . pretty different.

They seemed pretty different in the beginning. Um . . . the, oh . . . the only thing that I see here is that some of these lines don't seem to fit as well as others into what you're saying.

Ya. Ya that's right. Some, some of them I can't—

Some of them fit very well, and make a nice meaning. Some of them don't seem to fit in . . .

Clearly.

Um . . . I think it might be helpful, we've got a little extra time, if you want to just . . . read through it very quickly again and see if it falls into any different patterns of meaning besides that one.

Okay. Silently or out loud?

Oh, whichever you're comfortable with. I don't care.

Silently. (*laughs*)

Okay.

> (*long pause, reads silently*) Um . . . I think it's, ah . . . pretty much the same thing as I said before . . . basically what it's about I think is . . . you being in control of your life, . . . whatever is ahead . . . and you don't . . . know what it is if you're, you're yourself . . . and you're not afraid you'll just go ahead, take day by day.

Okay. Um, one last question that I have for you. How does the poem make you feel? You told me what you thought about it; how does it make you feel?

> Okay. Um . . . it makes me feel big. (*laughs*) It makes me feel . . . you know. . . like I can do whatever I put my mind to.

Okay. That's nice. Thank you.

David

Interviewer (*after the poem is read*): Do you have any questions about it?

> *David*: M-hmm. What's that "mosquito-doped"?

Okay, I—I presume it means um . . . having mosquito, you know, the lotion that you put on to repel the mosquitos? I don't know . . . "You, going along the path, mosquito-doped."

> The first thing I got was a—a cyclops. (*unclear*) You know . . . legendary cyclops walking through the forest but. . . sounds more like a train or something.

Okay. M-hmm. Any other feelings or thoughts about it besides . . . a general impression?

> He's huge, you know, there's, like . . . there's, everything's afraid of him.

M-hmm.

> (*pause*) He has no fear. Like he doesn't seem to be afraid just walking by himself.

Okay, why don't you read it silently now and, ah . . . think about it?

> (*v. long pause*)

Okay? You finished all the way through? Okay. Anything else you want to say about . . . what you're thinking now.

> Well . . . like, the way it's written in some parts . . . um . . . the engine. It's making a bristling noise.

M-hmm.

> Wait, ah . . .

Well, listen, ah, you seem to be going through it anyway, so why don't
you start at this point and read, read a stanza or so, and when you feel like
stopping just stop and let me know what it is you feel you're reading.
Okay? How it makes you feel and what you're thinking as you go along.

(*reads lines 1–6*) Okay, that first stanza, "going along the path" that's
. . . the tracks. "mosquito-doped" I'm not sure about that. "mosquito-
doped". . . Are . . . are mosquitoes attracted to light?

I guess most insects are attracted to light.

So there could be . . . bunch of mosquitoes around there. There's no
moon, it's a dark cloudy night. Well not cloudy, you can't tell yet.
"flashlight / a single orange eye." Okay, "unable to see what is beyond
/ the capsule of your dim sight," can't see beyond . . . where—what
. . . the . . . the light lights up?

M-hmm.

Okay, "what shape / contracts to a heart / with terror, bumps / among
the leaves, what makes / a bristling noise like a fur throat." What's hiding in the woods . . . what . . . what makes those noises?

M-hmm.

"Is it true you do not wish to hurt them?" Well . . . that's like . . .
you're just a train, I mean. They're . . . they're afraid. Why do they just
put one sentence at a time? Like . . . "Is it true you do not wish to hurt
them?" and, eh . . . "do not disguise / yourself in armour." Like they
cut it in half (*unclear*) sentence. "swim in their darkness as in a river /
do not disguise / yourself in armour" and it goes on.

Oh ya, I see what you mean. M-hmm.

Why; . . . why they have that? And in the end they—

So you're talking about the way. . . why it's structured the way it is. Why
she ends the sentence the same.

Yeah. Same . . . same thing at the end: "you are the hugest monster."
(*long pause*)

What are you saying about that line?

Like, you know it's structured differently, like, everything else just
stands out.

You mean that it's, it's on a separate line, it seems to be a stanza all by
itself, is that what you mean?

Ya. Ya. Stanza like . . . a stanza is pretty big. This might mean . . . like
this guy is really big, he doesn't need mu—you don't have to say much
about him.

Okay, who is "this guy" or . . . I'm not sure what you mean.

Well . . . it's. . . at first I thought it was a cyclops but it sounds more
like a . . . a train. 'Cause, okay, a flashlight, "a single orange eye." That

. . . most trains have a . . . a . . . big light on it. And, ah . . . okay, "unable to see [what is] beyond / the capsule of your dim / sight, what shape / contracts to a heart / with terror, bumps / among the leaves, what makes / a bristling noise like a fur throat." Like, that's the . . . of you 'cause they don't understand what—what it is. (*long pause*) Eh (*reads lines 12–13*). That, oh boy . . . the part about the shoes, the shoes . . . (*unclear*) "let your eyes go bare" Turn off the light? and "swim in their darkness as in a river" . . . just . . . go by. But I don't know . . . that part about the shoes, it's . . . puzzling.

Okay, so you—you . . . so far you've been puzzled over . . . um . . . mosquito-doped and, and the part about taking off the shoes. You want to finish?

Well taking off the shoes, that might be, um . . . like take off the shoes to be quiet, like when people take off their shoes. Like . . . they . . .

But how would that apply to a train?

I know . . . it's . . . it's hard, let's see, taking off the shoes, getting rid, no, can't be getting rid of cars. Um. (*pause*)

It's rather hard to fit in with the image. Go on and finish it and see how it—

(*reads lines 16–17*) This could be . . . um . . . the . . . engineer, inside the train, talking about now. Not, like . . . don't hide inside the train. (*reads lines 18–21*) Hmm . . . (*pause*) (*softly*) "chemical / smell" . . . "cold fire" . . . (*pause*) "chemical / smell" that's . . . that's puzzling (*laughs*) 'cause . . . trains . . . would—would coal be, ah . . . considered a chemical smell?

I don't know. I—I'm not sure what it means myself. I'm not sure . . . what does it make you think of?

"Chemical / smell" I . . . you know, something more scientific than a train. Makes me think . . . 'cause, eh . . . well, the picture I get . . . this is an old train, you know, the kind that runs on coal.

Where did you get the first image of the train? When did you stop in the reading of the poem?

Armour. As soon as I got to *armour*.

Oh, the word *armour*.

When you, when you were reading it . . . I thought, ah, it's a cyclops, you know . . . legendary cyclops. Then I saw *armour* and then, ah . . . "chemical / smell," "cold fire" . . .

Oh, that's where you got the train in the first place.

Ya.

Okay. Want to finish it all?

Ya. (*reads lines 22–23*) I think it's the . . . side of the train there, where the . . . wheels are. "where danger is not knowing, / you are the hugest monster." . . . You're not scared, well, it's a machine, it's not afraid of anything. And only . . . you could only scare the other people and . . . and the other animals. I don't think it . . .

What do you mean "the other animals"?

The animals in the forest.

Okay, but you said "other animals" You. . .

Well, there's . . . all kinds of animals. Well, according to this there's animals, uh . . . watching it. (*pause*) Let's see . . . um . . .

Does that make a lot of sense to you, that . . . that they would have, that . . . a train is frightening the animals? I mean . . . I'm just trying to put it all together. I'm wonder[ing] . . . what, what it all fits together . . . how it all fits together as a pattern.

Right. A train . . . most animals would run away.

M-hmm.

They wouldn't stay around. But there's a lot of . . . like here, "contracts to a heart / with terror, bumps / among the leaves, " like, that I can't see, I can't un—associate that with a train.

That's true. Yes. I see. And . . . "mosquito," that goes with "mosquito-doped" and . . . uh . . . what's the other one . . . that you had trouble with associating with the train? . . . Oh, shoes.

Shoes? (*pause*) "chemical / smell"—I don't . . . I don't think . . . "a cold fire" (*v. long pause*) Well "chemical / smell" that means . . . pungent, like most chemicals are very strong-smelling. So this could . . . what's a one-eyed monster? "single orange eye". . . It's not a train.

Start . . . go back and start at the very beginning. And . . . read it again. Try it again.

(*reads lines 1–3*)

Okay now, why don't you stop there . . . and tell me what you . . . see or hear or feel, what does that make you think, just that stanza?

Just . . . when I saw that . . . ah . . . a miner, you know mining?

Ah, yes.

Mining caps? they have one eye? One, eh . . . flashlight?

Yes. M-hmm.

(*reads lines 4–10*) M-hmm. That's getting . . . could be . . . "bumps / among the leaves" (*pause*) 'Course you haven't leaves in mines.

Maybe it's . . . maybe it's not in a mine, but the image of the miner is . . . is a nice image. It could be that.

"brist— eh, "fur throat." What would . . . that would be, like, eh . . . growling?

M-hmm.

Growling, type. (*reads lines 11–15*). Hmm. (*long pause*)

Say what you're thinking.

Um it's . . . the guy, you know, take off his un—hat, get rid of his un— eye, sight.

M-hmm.

(*laughs*) Take off his shoes. Be like a wild animal.

Yes. M-hmm. That seems to be it.

(*reads lines 16–17*) Don't wear clothes.
(*reads lines 18–21*) They don't under . . . stand. They can't.

Who's "they"?

The animals. The animals are watching from hiding. "chemical / smell" like to them . . . animals can smell . . . smell people because they . . . they're like the forest; they have . . . pungent odor.

M-hmm.

"cold fire" (*pause*) That I can't really seem to get. "you are / giant and indefinable." You're much larger than most of the animals. (*reads lines 22–24*) (*pause*)

M-hmm.

Let's see, "their monstrous night" No, that's the . . . I think that's a bunch of animals, over there, a monstrous night?

M-hmm.

That's where they get their claws "where danger is not knowing, / you are the hugest monster."

M-hmm?

(*v. long pause*)

Just say what you're thinking.

I could . . . I also get the . . . image of a hunter. Now . . . possibly some kind of threat to the animals. Maybe he has a gun or something.

Ah . . . for the . . . the image of the hunter as the . . . as what, as the . . . the *you* in the poem, is that what you're saying?

Ya. A hunter with a flashlight.

Oh, I see.

Or a lantern, no, flashlight. And (*pause*)

You can . . . you can go back and run through it again if you want.

Ya. There are so many . . . meanings.

(*laughs*) It's hard, I know . . . but there's the fun.

Ya.

Do you want, you want to run through it again, or—?

But . . . if it will be a hunter. . .

M-hmm.

Like, why do they put, "Is it true you do not wish to hurt them?" . . .
Unless he's just walking through the forest and wants to protect himself.

Aha, that's interesting.

"do not disguise / yourself in armour" That's . . . still clothes. I still
think it's clothes.

M-hmm.

(*v. long pause*)

I think it's helpful to—to keep reading it through, if you want to go back,
or . . . if you don't, you can just . . . skip around.

Well, hiding and all that . . . I still think it's the same thing as . . . they
could smell you . . . You're much bigger than most of the animals.
"Indefinable" . . . that's . . . they can't, what does that mean, indefinable? What's that? That's un—

Indefinable means you, you can't . . . define it or say exactly what it is.
You can't, eh . . . perhaps it means you can't understand it too well. I
don't know. Indefinable . . . something that's hard to understand would be
indefinable.

Ya. Can—animals don't understand. (*pause*) Ya, it—he's probably
walking in the wilds. Bu—there's . . . in the . . . in the wilds, there's
usually no path. Going back to the beginning.

There are no paths in the . . .

Well, usually. It's just overgrown. Except sometimes there's a rabbit
trail or something.

M-hmm.

(*v. long pause*) I'm going to go back to the beginning.

Okay.

"You, going along the path, / mosquito-doped, with no moon" . . . No
moon . . . it's really dark.

Okay.

"the flashlight, / a single orange eye." (*long pause*)

Say what you're thinking.

I don't know, I get . . . I get the . . . image, flashlight could be the sun
'cause . . . with no moon doesn't mean that . . . it has to be night.
'Cause the day there's no moon. But I don't know why I get that. It's
. . . it's, like, eh . . . just flashed in on me.

M-hmm. No, sure, that's, that's good though, you know . . . what it makes
you think of.

"a single orange eye" (*pause*) but then . . . "capsule of your dim /
sight" . . . It's got to be night. (*pause*) "Contracts" (*pause*) (*unclear*)

Ya. (*laughs*)

Put half a sentence here and half a sentence on the next stanza. (*reads
lines 4–10*). (*v. long pause*)

Just say what you're thinking.

Well, this person . . . according to the animals, must be . . . like, clumsy 'cause animals don't make that much noise when they're going
through the forest. "bumps / among the leaves" like he's clumsy.
"bumps" means clumsy . . . stepping all over the leaves. "what makes /
a bristling noise like a fur throat" . . . Doesn't necessarily have to be a
growl, could be . . . (*v. long pause*) That's puzzling.

(*laughs*) Okay.

(*v. long pause*) Ya, I think it is . . . a guy walking with, well, probably a
flashlight or possibly a miner . . . with a gun. Like, doesn't want to
hurt the people (*unclear*) Let's see, "Is it true you have no fear?" If he
didn't have fear, then he wouldn't use a gun . . . boy . . . it's getting . . .
making it more complicated.

(*laughs*) Just, I . . . it's helpful sometimes just to read the line, alone, as
you go along. You—I think you left one behind.

(*reads lines 11–15*) (*v. long pause*)

Oh, we're running out of time. You want to give me some last statements,
just . . . what you see in the poem as a whole?

Well, I . . . I just get this image of a . . . a person walking in a . . . a
forest. Man . . . I think it's man because . . . to animals man is like a
monster because he . . . he destroys and all that . . . builds . . . (*long
pause*) It's, ah . . . pretty . . . puzzling.

Um, in general. I'm just curious for my own benefit; do you like this kind
of poem or not?

Ya, it makes you think.

Makes you think?

Ya, and then you get all kinds of views. Especially the title, it's catchy
. . . like, personally, I like un—the deep little things on these, eh . . .
fantasy . . . eh, monsters (*unclear*) cyclops . . . caught my eye.

If you were reading this all by yourself, perhaps, without this kind of a situation, how would this kind of poem make you feel? I'm just curious.

I'd, I'd say this . . . well, I'd . . . probably think this is more like, ah . . . a cyclops itself. But most people . . . like . . . authors, they don't write about . . . mythological things . . . or . . . 'cause like the flashlight, the single orange eye, cyclops had one eye . . . and you can't see too far . . . except . . . beyond your own sight; and, okay, you're very large so you just step all over the leaves, you can't really avoid them. And when you breathe, that could be like a bristling noise. Like a fur throat. Yet you don't want to hurt them, you're just minding your own business . . . and here . . . you have no fear, I mean. . . you're so big . . . why should you be afraid of anything? (*reads lines 13–14*) Now that is . . . gets a bit puzzling. (*line 15*) I think that's . . . let yourself . . . go free. (*lines 16–17*) Don't put up a . . . front? I'm not sure about that. (*lines 18–21*). Well . . . there he's different. They sense that he's . . . he's. . . much different and . . . indefinable. They can't, they didn't understand because they've never ever seen this sort of thing. (*reads lines 22–25*) That last stanza . . . I think the reason they just put you are hugest . . . the hugest monster, is like . . . that's all, you don't need more explanation. As if you're you . . . you don't need a huge stanza to explain who you are.

Oh, that's interesting. That's good. Okay, thank you very much.

Bibliography

Resources on Teaching Poetry Reading and Writing

Andrews, R. 1991. *The Problem with Poetry*. Milton Keynes, England: Open University Press.

Beach, R., and J. Marshall. 1991. *Teaching Literature in Secondary Schools*. New York: Harcourt Brace Jovanovich.

Benton, M., and G. Fox. 1985. *Teaching Literature: Nine to Fourteen*. Oxford: Oxford University Press.

Benton, P. 1986. *Pupil, Teacher, Poem*. London: Hodder & Stoughton.

Blackie, P. 1971. "Asking Questions." *English in Education* 5, 3: 77–96.

Britton, J. 1993. *Literature in Its Place*. Portsmouth, NH: Heinemann.

Brownjohn, S. 1980. *Does It Have to Rhyme?* London: Hodder & Stoughton.

Creber, P. 1990. *Thinking Through English*. Milton Keynes, England: Open University Press.

Dias, P., and M. Hayhoe. 1988. *Developing Response to Poetry*. Milton Keynes, England: Open University Press.

Duke, C. R., and S. A. Jacobsen. 1992. *Poets' Perspectives*. Portsmouth, NH: Boynton/Cook.

Dunning, S., and W. Stafford. 1992. *Getting the Knack: 20 Poetry Writing Exercises*. Urbana, IL: National Council of Teachers of English.

Fox, G., and B. Merrick. 1981. "Thirty-Six Things to Do with a Poem." *Children's Literature in Education* 12, 1.

Graves, D. 1992. *Explore Poetry*. Portsmouth, NH: Heinemann.

Hayhoe, M., and S. Parker. 1988. *Words Large as Apples*. Cambridge: Cambridge University Press.

117

Heard, G. 1989. *For the Good of the Earth and the Sun.* Portsmouth, NH: Heinemann.

Hughes, T. 1967. *Poetry in the Making.* London: Faber & Faber.

Jackson, D. 1986. "Poetry and the Speaking Voice." *English in Education* 20, 2: 30–42.

Koch, K. 1970. *Wishes, Lies, and Dreams.* New York: Chelsea House.

Krogness, M. 1994. *Just Teach Me, Mrs. K.: Talking, Reading, and Writing with Reluctant Adolescent Learners.* Portsmouth, NH: Heinemann.

McKendy, T. 1987. "Arguing about Taste: An Introduction to Poetry." *English in Education* 21, 3.

Miller, J., ed. 1984. *Eccentric Propositions: Essays on Literature and the Curriculum.* London: Routledge & Kegan Paul.

Probst, R. E. 1986. *Response and Analysis: Teaching Literature in Junior and Senior High School.* Portsmouth, NH: Boynton/Cook.

Purves, A., T. Rogers, and A. Soter. 1990. *How Porcupines Make Love II: Teaching a Response-Centred Literature Curriculum.* New York: Longman.

Tchudi, S. and S. Tchudi. 1991. *The English/Language Arts Handbook: Classroom Strategies for Teachers.* 2d ed. Portsmouth, NH: Boynton/Cook.

Tsujimoto, J. L. 1988. *Teaching Poetry Writing to Adolescents.* Urbana, Ill.: National Council of Teachers of English.

References

Abercrombie, M. J. L. 1969. *The Anatomy of Judgment.* Harmondsworth, England: Penguin.

Afflerbach, P., and P. Johnston. 1984. "On the Use of Verbal Reports in Reading Research." *Journal of Reading Behavior* 16: 307–322.

Anderson, R. C. 1977. "The Notion of Schemata and the Educational Enterprise." *In Schooling and the Acquisition of Knowledge,* ed. R. C. Anderson, R. J. Spiro, and W. E. Montague. Hillsdale, NJ: Erlbaum.

Applebee, A. 1977. "The Elements of Response to a Literary Work: What We Have Learned." *Research in the Teaching of English* 11: 255–271.

———. 1978. *The Child's Concept of Story.* Chicago: University of Chicago Press.

Barnes, D. and D. Barnes. 1990. "Reading and Writing as Social Action." In *Developing Discourse Practices in Adolescence and Adulthood,* ed. R. Beach and S. Hynds, 34–64. Norwood, NJ: Ablex.

Barnes, D., J. Britton, and H. Rosen. 1971. *Language, the Learner, and the School.* Harmondsworth, England: Penguin.

Barnes, D., P. Churley, and C. Thompson. 1971. "Group Talk and Literary Response." *English in Education* 5, 3: 63–76.

Bartlett, F. C. 1932. *Remembering.* Cambridge: Cambridge University Press.

Beach, R. 1972. "The Literary Response Process of College Students While Reading and Discussing Three Poems." Ph.D. dissertation, University of Illinois at Urbana. *Dissertation Abstracts International*, 34, 656A.

———. 1993. *A Teacher's Introduction to Reader-Response Theories*. Urbana, Ill.: National Council of Teachers of English.

Beach, R., and S. Hynds. 1990. "Research on Response to Literature." In *Transactions with Literature: A Fifty-Year Perspective*, ed. E. J. Farrell and J. R. Squire, 131–205. Urbana, Ill.: National Council of Teachers of English.

———. 1991. "Research on Response to Literature." In *Handbook of Reading Research*, vol. 2, ed. R. Barr, M. Kamil, P. Mosenthal, and P. D. Pearson, 453–489. New York: Longman.

Belsey, C. 1980. *Critical Practice*. London: Methuen.

Benton, M., J. Teasey, R. Bell, and K. Hurst. 1988. *Young Readers Responding to Poems*. London: Routledge.

Bleich, D. 1975. *Readings and Feelings: An Introduction to Subjective Criticism*. Urbana, Ill.: National Council of Teachers of English.

———. 1978. *Subjective Criticism*. Baltimore: Johns Hopkins University Press.

Britton, J. N. 1954. "Evidence of Improvement in Poetic Judgment." *British Journal of Educational Psychology* 45: 196–208.

Brown, A. L. 1980. "Metacognitive Development and Reading." In *Theoretical Issues in Reading Comprehension: Perspectives from Cognitive Psychology, Linguistics, Artificial Intelligence, and Education*, ed. R. J. Spiro, B. C. Bruce, & W. J. Brewer. Hillsdale, NJ: Erlbaum.

Brown, G., and G. Yule. 1983. *Discourse Analysis*. Cambridge: Cambridge University Press.

Brubacher, M., R. Payne, and K. Rickett, eds. 1990. *Perspectives on Small Group Learning*. Oakville, ONT: Rubicon Publishing.

Bryant, C. 1984. "Teaching Students to Read Poetry Independently: An Experiment in Bringing Together Research and the Teacher." *English Quarterly* 17, 4: 48–57.

Ciardi, J. 1959. *How Does a Poem Mean?* Boston: Houghton Mifflin.

Cooper, C. 1971. "Measuring Appreciation of Literature: A Review of the Attempts." *Research in the Teaching of English* 5: 6–23.

———, ed. 1985. *Researching Response to Literature and the Teaching of Literature: Points of Departure*. Norwood, NJ: Ablex.

Cooper, M., and M. Holzman. 1983. "Talking about Protocols." *College Composition and Communication* 34: 248–296.

Culler, J. 1975. *Structuralist Poetics: Structuralism, Linguistics, and the Study of Literature*. London: Routledge & Kegan Paul.

———. 1981. *The Pursuit of Signs: Semiotics, Literature, Deconstruction*. London: Routledge & Kegan Paul.

D'Arcy, P. 1973. *Reading for Meaning*. vol. 2, The Reader's Response. London: Hutchison Educational.

Dias, P. 1979. "Developing Independent Readers of Poetry: An Approach in the High School." *McGill Journal of Education* 14: 199–214.

———.1992. "Literary Reading and Classroom Constraints: Aligning Practice with Theory." In *Literature Instruction: A Focus on Student Response*, ed. J. Langer., 131–162. Urbana, Ill.: National Council of Teachers of English.

van Dijk, T. 1980. "Story Comprehension: An Introduction." *Poetics* 9: 1–21.

Dillon, G. 1980. "Discourse Processing and the Nature of Literary Narrative." *Poetics* 9: 163 -180.

Dixon, J. 1974. "Formulation in Group Discussion." *Educational Review* (Birmingham) 26: 241–250.

Eagleton, T. 1983. *Literary Theory: An Introduction*. Oxford: Blackwell.

Eeds, M., and M. Wells. 1989. "Grand Conversations: An Experiment of Meaning Construction in Literature Groups." *Research in the Teaching of English* 23, 1: 4–29.

Engbrecht, R. 1986. "Individualizing Approaches to Poetry." In *English Teachers at Work: Strategies from Five Countries*, ed. S. Tchudi. Portsmouth, NH: Boynton/Cook.

Ericsson, K. A., and H. A. Simon. 1980. "Verbal Reports as Data." *Psychological Review* 87: 215–251.

———. 1984. *Protocol Analysis: Verbal Reports as Data*. Cambridge, Mass.: MIT Press.

Fish, S. 1980. *Is There a Text in This Class?* Cambridge, Mass.: Harvard University Press.

Flower, L., and J. Hayes. 1985. "Response to Marilyn Cooper and Michael Holzman, 'Talking about Protocols.'" *College Composition and Communication* 36: 94–99.

Goodman, K. 1967. "Reading: A Psycholinguistic Guessing Game." *Journal of the Reading Specialist* 6: 126–135.

Graves, D. H. 1981. "Renters and Owners: Donald Graves on Writing." *English Magazine* 8, 4–7.

Green, J., and D. Bloome. 1983. "Ethnography and Reading: Issues, Approaches, Criteria, and Findings." In *Searches for Meaning in Reading—Language Processing and Instruction*, ed. J. Niles and L. Harrison. Washington, D.C.: National Reading Conference.

Griffith, P. 1987. *Literary Theory and English Teaching*. Milton Keynes, England: Open University Press.

Grugeon, E., and P. Walden, eds. 1978. *Literature and Learning*. London: Ward Lock Educational.

Gumperz, J. 1982. *Discourse Strategies*. Cambridge: Cambridge University Press.

Harding, D. W. 1937. "The Role of the Onlooker." *Scrutiny* 6: 247–258.

———. 1963. *Experience into Words*. London: Chatto & Windus.

———. 1968. "Practice at Liking: A Study in Experimental Aesthetics." *Bulletin of the British Psychological Society* 21, 70: 3–10.

Harpin, W. S. 1966. "The Appreciation of Prose." *Educational Review* 19: 13–22.

Harste, J. C., and R. F. Carey. 1979. "Comprehension as Setting." In *New Perspectives on Comprehension*, ed. J. C. Harste and R. F. Carey, 4–22. Bloomington, Ind.: Indiana University Press.

Hayes, J. and L. Flower, 1980. "Identifying the Organization of Writing Processes." In *Cognitive Processes in Writing*, ed. L.W. Gregg and E.R. Steinberg, 3–30. Hillsdale, NJ: Erlbaum.

———. 1983. "Uncovering Cognitive Processes in Writing: An Introduction to Protocol Analysis." In *Research in Writing: Principles and Methods*, ed. P. Mosenthal, L. Tamor, and S. A. Walmsley, 207–220. New York: Longman.

Hayhoe, M. 1984. "Sharing the Headstart: An Exploratory Approach to Teaching Poetry." *English Quarterly* 17, 3: 39–44.

Holland, N. 1973. *Poems in Persons: An Introduction to the Psychoanalysis of Literature*. New York: W. W. Norton.

———. 1975. *Five Readers Reading*. New Haven, Conn.: Yale University Press.

Hunt, R. 1993. "Texts, Textoids, and Utterances: Writing and Reading for Meaning, in and out of Classrooms." In *Constructive Reading: Teaching Beyond Communication*, ed. S. Straw and D. Bogdan, 113–129. Portsmouth, NH: Boynton/Cook.

Iser, W. 1978. *The Act of Reading: A Theory of Aesthetic Response*. Baltimore: Johns Hopkins University Press.

Kantor, K., D. R. Kirby, and J. P. Goetz. 1981. "Research in Context: Ethnographic Studies in English Education." *Research in the Teaching of English* 15: 293–309.

Kintgen, E. 1983. *The Perception of Poetry*. Bloomington, Ind.: Indiana University Press.

Kintsch, W. 1980. "Learning from Text, Levels of Comprehension, or, Why Anyone Would Read a Story Anyway." *Poetics* 9: 87–98.

Klemenz-Belgardt, E. 1981. "American Research on Response to Literature: The Empirical Studies." *Poetics* 10: 357–380.

Knights, L. C. 1964. "In Search of Fundamental Values." In *The Critical Moment: Literary Criticism in the 1960s* (Essays from the *London Times Literary Supplement*), 75–81. New York: McGraw-Hill.

Langer, J., ed. 1992. *Literature Instruction: A Focus on Student Response*. Urbana, Ill.: National Council of Teachers of English.

Langer, J., and M. Smith-Burke, eds. 1982. *Reader Meets Author—Bridging the Gap: A Psycholinguistic and Sociolinguistic Perspective*. Newark, Del.: International Reading Association.

Langer, S. K. 1953. *Feeling and Form*. New York: Charles Scribner's Sons.

LATE (London Association of Teachers of English). 1968. *Assessing Comprehension*. London: Blackie.

Leavis, F. R. 1948. *Education and the University*. London: Chatto & Windus.

———. 1962. *Two Cultures? The Significance of C. P. Snow*. London: Chatto & Windus.

———. 1963. *The Common Pursuit*. Harmondsworth, England: Penguin.

MacLean, M. 1985. "A Framework for Analyzing Reader-Text Interactions." *Journal of Research and Development in Education* 19, 2: 16–21.

Mailloux, S. 1982. *Interpretive Conventions*. Ithaca, NY: Cornell University Press.

McDermott, R. 1977. "The Ethnography of Speaking and Reading." In *Linguistic Theory: What Can It Say about Reading?* ed. R. Shuy. Newark, Del.: International Reading Association.

McHoul, A. 1978. "Ethnomethodology and Literature: Preliminaries to a Sociology of Reading." *Poetics* 7: 113–120.

Mellon, J. C. 1975. *National Assessment and the Teaching of English*. Urbana, Ill.: National Council of Teachers of English.

Mills, R. W. 1974. "Small Group Discussion." *English in Education* 8: 10–21.

Minsky, M. 1975. "A Framework for Representing Knowledge." In *The Psychology of Computer Vision*, ed. P. H. Winston. New York: McGraw-Hill.

Mishler, E. G. 1986. *Research Interviewing*. Cambridge, Mass.: Harvard University Press.

Moffett, J. 1968. *Teaching the Universe of Discourse*. Boston: Houghton Mifflin.

National Assessment of Educational Progress. 1973. *Literature: Responding to Literature*. Report 02-102. Washington, DC: U.S. Government Printing Office.

———. 1981. *Reading, Thinking, and Writing—Results from the 1979–80 National Assessment of Reading and Literature*. Report 1 1-L-01. Denver, Colo.: National Assessment of Educational Progress.

Olshavsky, J. E. 1976/77. "Reading as Problem-Solving: An Investigation of Strategies." *Reading Research Quarterly* 124: 654–674.

Purves, A. 1979. "That Sunny Dome: Those Caves of Ice: A Model for Research in Reader Response." *College English* 407: 802–812.

Purves, A., A Foshay, and G. Hansson. 1973. *Literature Education in Ten Countries: An Empirical Study*. Stockholm: Almqvist & Wiksell.

Purves, A., and R. Beach. 1972. *Literature and the Reader: Research in Response to Literature, Reading Interests, and the Teaching of Literature*. Urbana, Ill.: National Council of Teachers of English.

Purves, A., with V. Rippere. 1968. *Elements of Writing about a Literary Work: A Study of Response to Literature*. Urbana, Ill.: National Council of Teachers of English.

Richards, I. A. 1929. *Practical Criticism*. New York: Harcourt, Brace and World.

Rosenblatt, L. 1938. *Literature as Exploration*. New York: Appleton-Century.

————. 1978. *The Reader, the Text, the Poem: The Transactional Theory of the Literary Work*. Carbondale, Ill.: Southern Illinois University Press.

————. 1982. "The Literary Transaction: Evocation and Response." *Theory into Practice* 21, 4: 268–277.

————. 1985. "Viewpoints: Transaction Versus Interaction—A Terminological Rescue Operation." *Research in the Teaching of English* 19: 96–107.

Rumelhart, D. E. 1984. "Understanding Understanding." In *Understanding Reading Comprehension*, ed. J. Flood, 1–20. Newark, Del.: International Reading Association.

Sanford, A. J., and S. C. Garrod. 1981. *Understanding Written Language*. Chichester, England: Wiley.

Schank, R. C., and R. Abelson. 1977. *Scripts, Plans, Goals, and Understanding*. Hillsdale, NJ: Erlbaum.

Silkey, S., and A. Purves. 1973. "What Happens When We Read a Poem." *Journal of Aesthetic Education* 7, 3: 63–72.

Slatoff, W. 1970. *With Respect to Readers: Dimensions of Literary Response*. Ithaca, NY: Cornell University Press.

Smagorinsky, P. 1989. "The Reliability and Validity of Protocol Analysis." *Written Communication* 6: 463–479.

Smith, F. 1978. *Understanding Reading*. 2d ed. New York: Holt, Rinehart & Winston.

————. 1983. "Reading Like a Writer." *Language Arts* 60, 5: 558–567.

Spiro, R. J. 1979. "Etiology of Reading Comprehension Style." In *Reading Research Studies and Applications*, ed. M. Kamil and A. Moe, 118–122. Twenty-eighth Yearbook of the National Reading Conference. Clemson, SC: National Reading Conference.

————. 1980. "Prior Knowledge and Story Processing: Integration, Selection, and Variation." *Poetics* 9: 313–327.

————. 1982. "Long-term Comprehension: Schema-based Versus Experiential and Evaluative Understanding." *Poetics* 11: 77–86.

Spiro, R. J., B. C. Bruce, and W. J. Brewer, eds. 1980. *Theoretical Issues in Reading Comprehension: Perspectives from Cognitive Psychology, Linguistics, Artificial Intelligence, and Education*. Hillsdale, NJ: Erlbaum.

Squire, J. 1964. *The Responses of Adolescents while Reading Four Short Stories*. Urbana, Ill.: National Council of Teachers of English.

Stratta, L., J. Dixon, and A. Wilkinson. 1973. *Patterns of Language: Explorations in the Teaching of English*. London: Heinemann Educational Books.

Straw, S. 1989. "Collaborative Learning and Response to Theme in Poetry." *Reading—Canada—Lecture* 7: 191–200.

Suleiman, S. R. and I. Crossman, eds. 1980. *The Reader in the Text: Essays on Audience and Interpretation*. Princeton, NJ: Princeton University Press.

Tompkins, J. P., ed. 1980. *Reader-response Criticism: From Formalism to Post-struc-turalism.* Baltimore: Johns Hopkins University Press.

Torbe, M. 1974. "Modes of Response: Some Interactions between Reader and Literature." *English in Education* 8: 21–32.

Travers, D. M. 1982. "Problems in Writing about Poetry and Some Solutions." *English in Education* 16, 3: 55–65.

———. 1984. "The Poetry Teacher: Behavior and Attitudes." *Research in the Teaching of English* 18: 367–384.

Vipond, D., and R. A. Hunt. 1984. "Point-driven Understanding: Pragmatic and Cognitive Dimensions of Literary Reading." *Poetics* 13: 261–277.

Waern, Y. 1979. *Thinking Aloud During Reading: A Descriptive Model and Its Application.* Psychology Department Report No. 546. Stockholm: University of Stockholm.

Weisberg, R. 1979. "A Comparison of Good and Poor Readers' Ability to Comprehend Explicit and Implicit Information in Short Stories Based on Two Modes of Presentation." *Research in the Teaching of English* 13: 337–351.

Willinsky, J. 1990. *The New Literacy: Redefining Reading and Writing in the Schools.* New York: Routledge.

Young, R. 1986. "Theme in Fictional Literature: A Way into Complexity." In *The Territory of Language: Linguistics, Stylistics, and the Teaching of Composition,* ed. D. McQuade, 313–323. Carbondale, Ill.: Southern Illinois University Press.